What Others Are Saying...

"A wonderful financial tutorial which toggles nicely between a roller coaster metaphor and some cold, hard facts. Everyone should read the Money Ride."
—Joseph Engelberg, Ph.D.
Assistant Professor of Finance
University of North Carolina

"A compelling explanation of how, throughout life, one can make better decisions about money... Without insulting our intelligence he makes certain that even the most elementary issues are understood... A most enjoyable and illuminating ride!"
—Richard Farson, author, psychologist
President, Western Behavioral Sciences Institute

"As economic cycles come and go this book will hold up as a primer for anyone who wants to understand the basics of wealth accumulation and preservation. *The Money Ride* enhances money intelligence and money behavior."
—Vaughn Woods, CFP, MBA

"Much more than a how-to-balance-a-checkbook book, *The Money Ride* provides an excellent road map for developing a clear perspective on the key factors of life including, but not limited to, money."
—Ed Blitz, CPA, author
The 10% Solution-Your Key to Financial Security

The Money Ride

TMR

A Passenger's Guide to Money & Wealth

William K. Busch

illustrations by Dennis L. Busch

2016
KALA PUBLISHING
LA JOLLA, CALIFORNIA

ISBN 978-0-9826393-6-8

Type design by Studio E Books, Santa Barbara, California

Published by Kala Publishing
7514 Girard Avenue #1727
La Jolla, CA 92037
www.themoneyride.com

Acknowledgments

I have not attempted to cite in the text all of the sources consulted in writing this book. To do so would require more pages than would be practical. The list would include government departments, periodicals, colleagues and experts in the fields of economics, finance, real estate, investing and psychology.

Many people contributed to this book, and two people in particular contributed to its classroom development: David Jones and Joseph Cavaiola. They have allowed me to work with their students to develop the Money Ride concepts and test the effectiveness of the teaching approach.

A special thanks to Bill Butler whose patience and help with writing and editing was vital, Dennis Busch for illustrating, Eric Larson for the book design and Doug Burgett for the cover design.

Finally, most important of all…to Diane, Josef and Julia—thanks to your love, support and encouragement, *The Money Ride* keeps on rolling!

Contents

The
Money
Ride

Introduction

Have you ever been to an amusement park? If you have, did you find the Money Ride? If you didn't, you missed the most amazing ride of them all! But don't feel bad if you missed it, because you're not the only one.

The Money Ride is hard to find, by design. It isn't noisy and flashy like the other rides. It's just a giant, plain, box-looking building with an entrance marked "$TART" at one side and an exit marked "FINI$H" at the other side.

It's what's inside the Money Ride that makes it the most exciting, scariest and longest ride in the park!

Inside, there's a wind tunnel containing a huge roller coaster with trillions of dollar bills swirling all around you. The fantastic thing about the Money Ride is that from the time you enter until you exit *you get to use and enjoy all the money you grab!*

This book shows you how you can get on the Money Ride and make the most of your trip. As you read these pages, you will learn how to effectively manage and grow your money to create the life you want to live. The valuable, easy-to-remember money tools and tips will help you take advantage of every up, down, twist and turn.

You will not be alone on your Money Ride adventure. Along the way, you will meet some of your fellow passengers and learn from their good and bad money decisions. Observing their choices will help you create and sustain sound money habits that will enable you to live a happier, more prosperous life. So, buckle up and get ready to enjoy the Money Ride—it's the ride of a lifetime and we are all on it!

I. The Ride

Welcome!

Welcome to the Money Ride! This book is your passenger guide for making your turn on the ride an unforgettable adventure.

As you wait in line, eager for your turn to begin, you can only imagine what it's going to be like. How wild and radical can the roller coaster ride be? And what about all that money swirling about—all for the taking? You're getting more and more excited as you visualize all the money you're going to grab and all the stuff you're going to be able to buy.

The line shuffles forward and soon you can hear the shouting, screaming and laughter as the people ahead of you disappear behind the big door labeled "$TART."

While you wait, you're frantically thumbing the pages of your passenger guide searching for every advantage you can give yourself once you get inside. The more you read the more you begin to realize that this concept of "use and enjoy all the money you grab" probably won't be as free and easy as it sounds—and you're right.

Like most rides at the amusement park, the Money Ride has rules that you must follow. But unlike the other rides, the rules are not about how old you are, how big you are or even about keeping your arms inside the car.

On the Money Ride the rules influence how much money you will be able to grab—these are called the "Grabbing Rules." We will cover these rules shortly, but first we're going to talk about how you can make the most of your turn on the Money Ride.

Making the Most of Your Turn

The Money Ride is called "The Ride of a Lifetime" because your pursuit of financial success is a lifelong adventure.

This passenger guide provides you with information on the basic rules and dynamics of money. Because the basic rules and dynamics of money and wealth do not change, they serve as a reliable foundation for making smart money decisions and achieving financial success.

Each passenger on the Money Ride has his or her own personal definition of what it means to be financially successful. Their definitions are unique, but they all describe a particular quality of life.

Your definition describes what your life will feel like once you have achieved financial success in terms of happiness, health, security, and freedom. This guide will help you develop the money behavior and skills required to create the money and wealth you will need to live that life.

Regardless of how you define financial success, your success will be determined by what you know about money and how you behave with money—knowing and doing. There are tips and tools throughout this guide that cover what you need to know and do to make the most of your turn on the Money Ride.

The interplay between knowing and doing influences your financial decisions, and if you want to realize its benefits you must do two things: (1) Learn the simple time-tested rules and dynamics of money described in this guide; and (2) apply the rules and dynamics to build and sustain sound money habits. Sound money habits are routines you use to process your money in ways that help you live a happier, more successful life.

The key is not just to read the money principles, tips and tools in this guide, but to use them to guide your money behavior with sound money habits. Sound money habits will then enable you to become financially self-reliant. Financial self-reliance means controlling your money so that you don't have to rely on others to give you the money you need to live your life. For most people, it is the prerequisite for achieving financial success, because if you don't first learn to control your money, your money will control you. Financial self-reliance is your first objective because it enhances your chances for financial stability and prosperity.

So, the sooner you begin to develop sound money habits, the sooner you will begin to reap the full rewards of your adventure on the Money Ride.

 Passenger Tips & Tools #1

Sound Money Habits

A habit consists of three parts, the Trigger, Routine and Reward. The trigger stimulates action, the routine consists of specific action steps and the reward is the emotion evoked by completing the routine.

For example, with the bad money habit of stupid spending ($-S^2$), the trigger is any situation that tempts you to buy something you don't need or can't afford. The routine is your step-by-step reaction to the temptation to spend. The reward is the fun of buying something, even though the purchase represents stupid spending ($-S^2$).

Here is an example of how you can create a new habit of smart spending ($+S^2$) to displace the destructive habit of stupid spending ($-S^2$):

1. Identify the situations or circumstances that act as your spending trigger.
2. Imagine your reward—the positive impact on your life resulting from the new habit.
3. Build a new routine of positive action steps to replace the old negative routine.
4. Practice, practice, practice your new routine when your triggers occur!

Start small, working on one habit routine at time. Be patient, it will take time for your new routines to become habit, but your happiness, financial self-reliance and success will be worth the effort.

2. The Rules

The Grabbing Rules

From the time you enter through the $tart door to the time you exit through the Fini$h door you get to use and enjoy all the money you grab. How much money you grab will depend upon these rules:

1. **If you don't graduate from high school.** You must keep your hands in your pockets and use only your teeth, elbows and knees to grab dollars.

2. **If you graduate from high school.** You are allowed to take your hands out of your pockets to grab more dollars.

3. **If you earn an AA degree or learn a marketable skill/trade.** You are given a small butterfly net to grab more dollars.

4. **If you earn a BA/BS degree.** You are given a medium-size butterfly net to grab still more dollars.

5. **If you earn a MA/MS degree.** You are given a large butterfly net to grab still more dollars.

6. **If you earn a PhD, MD or JD.** You are given a giant butterfly net to grab still more dollars.

7. **If you are a business owner.** You are given a giant butterfly net. You're also allowed to bring your employees on the ride with you and you get a bonus dollar for every dollar your employees grab.

As you study these Grabbing Rules you can see a connection between your ability to grab dollars and your level of formal education. It's as if you actually get paid to go to school.

"Can't be true," you say? Well it is true and there is data to prove it. Each year, the government keeps track of what everybody in the U.S. earns and spends...how and where they earn it and spend it.

The government data examine different aspects of earning and spending, looking for trends and connections between the two. One of the connections is the relationship between a person's education level and their earnings.

The government survey data compares the median earnings for seven levels of educational advancement, from high school drop out to advanced academic degrees. The data shows an increase in earnings with each advance in education level. Based on a decade of data and assuming a 40-year work career, the increase in earnings from one level to the next can be $300,000 or more—*the more you learn, the more you earn.* If you want to learn more about economic statistics, here are two U.S. government agencies that produce the data: (1.) The Bureau of Labor Statistics (www.bls.gov); and (2.)The Census Department (www.census.gov).

Once you've seen the data supporting the connection between education and income, go back to the question, do you actually get paid to go to school?

We essentially get paid for the time we are in school in a way similar to how professional athletes and CEOs of large corporations receive some of their pay...it's called *"deferred income."*

Deferred income is pay you receive at some point in the future after you have done the work according to some acceptable standard. The government data suggests that you really do get paid at some point in the future for the time and effort you spend educating yourself.

🎢 Passenger Tips & Tools #2

Do you know someone who is thinking about dropping out of high school or who actually has dropped out of high school? Well, if you do, go to that person and tell them that you know someone who will pay them $300,000 if they will just hang in there and get their high school diploma.

U.S. Government data show that assuming a 40-year working career, a person with no more than a high school diploma will earn an average of approximately $300,000 more than a high school dropout.

Your Work I.Q.

Your Work I.Q. is all of the education, work skills and personal skills you acquire that enable you to earn an income. There is no guarantee that a diploma or degree alone will translate to more income. The data show the advantage of the education—income connection, but hidden in the data is the equal importance of skill. Earning power is a product of what you know and what you know how to do—education and skill.

You really get paid to acquire knowledge and skills which are marketable—knowledge and skills which employers and customers need or want and will pay for. This means that your Work I.Q. is really your *work product*, consisting of your education, work skills and personal attributes which enable you to be a productive worker.

Education and work skills, as they relate to a particular job, are easy to define. Personal skills, on the other hand, are more general in their application and are important in all types of work. Personal skills consist of two basic aspects: people skills and work ethic.

Your people skills enable you to interact with your superiors, fellow workers and customers in a positive manner. On the Money Ride, no matter how smart or well trained you are, you will never reach your full grabbing potential without people skills.

Your work ethic defines what kind of worker you are—it is your attitude and approach to your work. The stronger your work ethic, the more reliable and productive a worker you will be.

How much you can sell your work product for depends upon the demand for it and your competition. The better paying the job, the more competition you will face.

You will compete for jobs against your fellow passengers, initially based upon your education, work skills and work experience. When these fail to give you a competitive advantage, your personal attributes may mean the difference. In these cases, your work ethic will help set you apart from your competition.

 Passenger Tips & Tools #3

What kind of worker are you?

Business owners know that when it comes to hiring workers…"Good people are hard to find."

If you want to be a worker in demand, be the kind of worker you would hire if you were a business owner.

Here are three simple but important things you can do to make yourself a valued employee to a business:

1. Be on time
2. Do what you say you are going to do.
3. Communicate clearly in spoken and written word.

As a passenger, you can only optimize your grabbing opportunities if your Work I.Q. has value, purpose and focus. The actual dollar value of your Work I.Q. is determined by employer demand for your specific *work product*. The purpose and focus of your Work I.Q. enhances your ability to identify and compete for available job and career opportunities. Purpose and focus also fuel a strong work ethic, making you a valued employee.

Like most passengers on the Money Ride, you will likely have many different jobs during your turn. It may take a lot of job sampling before you find the field or job that best suits you. Don't be afraid to try new job experiences—they are an important part of developing your Work I.Q.

Thanks to technology, you will have many job and career opportunities to choose from on the Money Ride. New industries emerge every year, needing educated workers with versatile skills. Be bold, conscientious, enthusiastic, determined and persistent in your pursuit.

As your Work I.Q. and productivity continue to grow, you will always be in demand. Remember that if you have value, purpose and focus, the more you can learn...the more you can earn.

Your Money I.Q.

No matter how developed your Work I.Q. is, it will only take you so far on the Money Ride.

If you really want to enjoy a successful financial life, you need to realize that your income is only the raw material of financial success.

The key to making the most of your turn on the Money Ride

will be your ability to create wealth by dynamically deploying the income that you grab. This will require a type of intelligence which is different from your Work I.Q., and it's called your "Money I.Q."

Your Money I.Q. consists of two parts:

1. Your knowledge and understanding of how money works.
2. Your ability to successfully apply that knowledge to a lifetime of money opportunities and challenges.

Work I.Q. generates income in the form of Grabbing Dollars, whereas Money I.Q. deploys income in the form of smart money decisions to pay for lifestyle and to create wealth. Wealth is property you own that can be sold to generate cash and property that also generates income without being sold.

While there is a direct connection between Work I.Q. and income, there is no such connection between Work I.Q. and wealth.

The amount of wealth you acquire during your turn on the Money Ride will therefore be influenced more by your Money I.Q., than by your Work I.Q.

The dynamics of Work I.Q. and Money I.Q. are covered later in this guide. Keep reading, and by the time your turn on the Money Ride begins, you'll have a solid foundation of money knowledge to help you make the most of the opportunities to turn your Grabbing Dollars into wealth.

3. Money Dynamics

The Roles of Money

You're getting really close now! So close that you can hear the roar of the roller coaster, feel the wind escaping from under the $TART door and you can even smell the money! There's not much time, so you need to carefully read these next few pages in your passenger's guide, because it's important that you learn "Money Dynamics" before you start your turn.

Money Dynamics consist of two important aspects of money which you must understand if you want to make the most of your ride: the Roles of Money and the Rules of Money. How much success you enjoy on the Money Ride will depend on your ability to understand and apply these two dynamics through your Money I.Q.

Each of the dollars that you will grab during your turn on the Money Ride will serve one or more of the following basic roles of money:

1. **Medium of Exchange.** This is the first, most important and most valuable use of money—buying stuff. Money is the primary exchange commodity used for all purchases and sales. The economy originally operated on the barter system, where you traded commodities like pigs and corn for other goods and services. But since pigs and corn come in different types and sizes, it was difficult to standardize the value of units being traded. Also, it was difficult to divide pigs and corn into smaller units, making it a real challenge to make change!

   To solve the problem of standard value and divisibility, the pigs and corn were replaced with a different trading commodity, currency—pieces of paper (dollars) with a standard value. So, when it comes to buying and selling stuff, dollars are like paper substitutes for pigs and corn.

Whether it's stuff you need or stuff you want, the ability to trade dollars for goods, services and property is what makes things happen on the Money Ride.

2. **Measure of Price or Value.** When you buy something, price is the impact on your current money supply, and cost is the impact on your future money supply—today's spending versus tomorrow's wealth. Value is a measure of current or potential market worth—the dollar amount for which something can be bought or sold. How much does it cost, and how much is it worth? Can you afford it? Is it a fair price or good deal? On the Money Ride all of these questions are answered in dollar units.

3. **Units for Storing Wealth.** How much is all your stuff worth? In this role, the dollar is used as the measure of how much wealth you accumulate in the form of stuff that you own. It also measures how the value of your wealth changes over time.

All your stuff is generally called "property," which consists of personal property and assets. Assets are special because they represent "wealth." An asset is either property that grows in value and is intended to be sold eventually in order to generate income, or it is property that generates income on its own without having to be sold.

On the Money Ride, the dollar is the measure of how much wealth you are creating and whether your wealth is growing or decaying as you roll along.

4. **Display of Wealth.** The value of a dollar can also be used to show people how much wealth you have. It can be in the form of expensive, flashy cars, huge homes, fancy clothing and jewelry or other property which gives the impression to other passengers that you have lots of money and wealth.

So, now that you know the four important roles of money, how do you think and feel about each of the roles money plays? Which role do you think has the most influence over your money decisions?

How you answer these questions about money tells you something about the kind of "Money Person" you are.

What kind of Money Person are you? On the Money Ride there are two basic types of Money Person: Spender and Saver. Regardless of which one you are, it is important that you know how the Money Person in you influences your financial decisions and behavior. The influence can be helpful or harmful to your financial success and the well-being of others who may rely on you for financial support. It is not about guilt, it is about developing sound money habits that are meaningful and practical.

It is not about judging yourself or others. You may find yourself behaving like a different type at different times—that's okay as long as you are aware of how your thinking affects your actions. Your ability to change your thinking and behavior will enable you to establish and maintain sound money habits which will enhance your chances for financial success.

Meet Your Fellow Passengers

Watching your fellow passengers on the Money Ride will help you reflect on your thinking and behavior. Watching them will allow you to reflect on your own money behavior. You are about to meet four passengers each of whom represents a type of behavior related to the use of money. You will be able to learn from seeing how they deploy the dollars they manage to grab.

Every passenger on the Money Ride uses money as a medium of exchange, but how they go about it differs based on their attitudes about money—how they relate to money. You will see some of yourself in them, as the Money Person they are influences their money decisions.

So, let's take a moment to meet some of the people who will be on the ride with you.

Suzie Spender. Suzie is a free-spender. To her, every dollar she grabs on the Money Ride "is meant to be spent." As soon as a dollar hits Suzie's hands the temptation to spend it grabs hold and dominates her money decisions.

Franklin Frugal. Franklin is a spender and a saver. He is a super shopper whose money behavior is driven by price and value. He understands the difference between price and cost and knows value when he sees it. He is always on the lookout for good deals and bargains that enable him to consistently spend less than he earns.

Sonya Stockpiler. Sonya is a saver. Having lots of money stashed away is really what drives Sonya's money decisions. She loves her units of stored value and keeps a close watch on how much money she has and where it is stockpiled. Sonya carefully watches every dollar she grabs and tries to stash as many dollars as she can in savings and investments.

Freddy Flash. Freddy is a spender and saver driven by status. He is really proud of his wealth and he is not shy about telling or showing people how wealthy he is. He just likes to show people he's wealthy by wearing flashy clothes and jewelry, driving expensive cars or living in an exclusive neighborhood.

You will want to be sure to look for Suzie, Franklin, Sonya and Freddy as you rumble along grabbing and stashing dollars. As you watch them you will learn some valuable lessons which will help you make the most of every dollar you grab.

Passenger Tips & Tools #4

Goals and Objectives

The terms "goals" and "objectives" are often used interchangeably, but there is a clear and simple difference between them. A goal is the destination and objectives are the progressive steps to getting to your destination. For example, if you need $600 six months from now, your goal is having the $600 six months from now. To make progress toward your goal, your objective becomes saving at least $100 every month.

Use the S.M.A.R.T. technique described later in this guide to establish money goals and map your path to achieving goals by establishing objectives/step to complete like stepping stones leading to the goal.

The Rules of Money

Money is not as complicated as most people think. You only have to remember three basic rules as you make money decisions and choices.

Rule 1: PAW and MAW

On the Money Ride, there are only two ways to make money: PAW and MAW. PAW dollars are the hourly wages or monthly salary you earn at work. PAW dollars are called "earned income."

MAW dollars are used to build wealth in assets like savings and investments. The income generated by your MAW dollars is called "passive income." The earned income from PAW and passive income from MAW are cash that flows into your life/personal economy called "cash flow." Cash flow is discussed in more detail later.

PAW is your Work I.Q. in action. Action is the key word here because it is not enough to simply grow and nurture your Work I.Q. You must put it into action and sustain your PAW activity with consistency and discipline—it's called your work ethic.

Be aware!—there are plenty of passengers on the Money Ride who seem to have a high Work I.Q., but who don't manage to get much grabbing done. They may be educated, creative, personable etc., but they never muster the ambition, drive or discipline needed to make the action part of PAW happen. They miss out on the financial opportunities that come from optimizing their Work I.Q./ PAW potential. You can't be this type of passenger *and* expect to make the most of your opportunities on the Money Ride.

As you master the dynamic of PAW, you will be able to create opportunities to use your MAW dynamic to grow wealth. MAW is really your Money I.Q. in action.

There will be numerous opportunities to build wealth during your turn on the Money Ride. Each opportunity will feature both promise and pitfalls…without both there would be no adventure! You will grow with every PAW and MAW decision you make, as you learn to recognize and optimize your Money Ride opportunities.

Rule 2: Money Is Limited

This rule is based upon a basic law of economics called the "Law of Scarcity." This law states that as an individual you have a limited money supply with which to try and fulfill a lifetime of needs and wants. You have to decide how each dollar is used and know that once you decide, you exclude all other possible uses for that dollar. This means that every important decision can have a positive or negative ripple effect on everything from your current cash flow to your long-term financial goals. Regardless of whether the impact is large or small, the ripple effect is present in every financial decision.

This law is universal and everyone—from the poor to the wealthy—must play by its rules. The basic difference between the poor and the wealthy is that the poor person's limited money resources are often "not enough" to cover needs and wants while the wealthy person's limited supply is usually "more than enough."

On the Money Ride, your ultimate goal is to efficiently manage your finances so that your limited money supply is always "more than enough" money for lifetime needs and wants.

The impact of every dollar choice you make is like the energy created by throwing a rock into a pond of liquid dollars. The rock represents a financial decision and the splash it makes is the initial impact of the decision on your personal finances.

But the splash also creates ripples which radiate outward, moving all the dollars in the pond. Some of the dollars may leave the pond, while the rest remain in the water moving with the ripples. The more important the decision, the bigger the rock and the more active the ripples.

The splash and ripples of financial decisions can affect efforts to manage cash flow and build wealth. That's why it is important to pay attention to both the splash and the ripples of every important financial decision.

Remember the Law of Scarcity. Your lifetime money supply consists of a limited number of dollars, each with its own potential. Make the most of your first-time opportunity with each dollar and pay attention to the ripple effect.

Rule 3: Money & Time

There is a fundamental and powerful connection between money and time, which causes your Money Ride dollars to grow or decay

in number and value over time. This growing and decaying is connected to another basic economic principle: The Time Value of Money.

There is a financial formula for calculating the change in money's value over time called the "Time Value of Money" formula. It is used to measure the growth and decay of money over time.

Keep in mind that math formulas are most useful for accurately measuring past changes in the value of money over time. They can also be used to project or estimate future changes in the value of money over time, but no formula can accurately predict the future value of your money—a projection is not a prediction.

The connection between time and money creates two basic kinds of time-connected money and on the Money Ride we call these "Today Dollars" and "Tomorrow Dollars."

 Passenger Tips & Tools #5

Time Value of Money Formula:
$$FV = P(1+i)^n$$

This formula can be used to measure the growth and the decay of money over time. Let's first look at how it is used to measure the decay of money. You'll learn how to use it to measure growth later in this guide.

FV	= Future value
P	= Present value/principal
i	= Interest rate
n	= Number of time periods

Using this formula, if you had $100 today (P) and you estimate that inflation will average –3% (i) over the next 20 years (n), what will be the future purchasing value (FV) in 20 years of your $100?

You can calculate the estimate that your $100 will have the purchasing power of $54.38 in today dollars…inflation decay of over 45% in 20 years!

Today Dollars are dollars that are available for immediate needs or wants. Today Dollars are a product of income. Today Dollars can come from PAW earnings, MAW savings and investments or from borrowing/debt. To be financially self-reliant, you must avoid using debt to generate Today Dollars for immediate needs and wants.

Tomorrow Dollars are dollars which need to be available for future needs and wants. Tomorrow Dollars are a product of wealth.

Each has its own particular purpose and importance in your Money Ride choices and decisions. This means that when you spend Today Dollars, it will be important to always be aware of the need to accumulate Tomorrow Dollars.

Understanding the difference between price and cost and recognizing the impact of the Ripple Effect will help you maintain a proper balance in your supply of Today Dollars and Tomorrow Dollars.

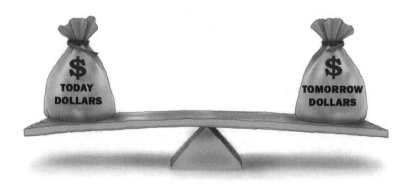

PAW and MAW

On the Money Ride the good and bad potential of the relationship between time and money is always at work, operating through two basic money dynamics: the "PAW Dynamic" and the "MAW Dynamic."

The PAW dynamic is about harvesting—grabbing Money Ride dollars. PAW's impact on your financial success will quickly become obvious to you in your grabbing efforts as you apply your Work I.Q. to gather as many dollars as you can.

It won't be enough to just work hard at the grabbing, you'll have to learn to work smart at the grabbing as well. Working smart makes the work less difficult and more productive.

The MAW dynamic is about storing and utilizing your harvest of PAW dollars. You will learn to make smart money decisions with your crop of fresh PAW dollars to create a continuous supply of MAW dollars for wealth building.

Efficiency is just as important in utilizing your MAW dollars as it is in harvesting PAW dollars. This is where your Money I.Q. will take over the stewardship of your wealth building efforts. Your financial success will ultimately be determined by how and where you apply your MAW dollars to create wealth.

The PAW and MAW dynamics both have the potential to cause your lifetime money supply to grow. Both are also vulnerable to economic forces and events whose impact can cause your lifetime money supply to decay.

This positive and negative potential is influenced by the Law of Scarcity, the Time Value of Money and the fact that money is a commodity.

Money Growth

Growth is the product of opportunities to increase earned income and accumulate wealth. Growth opportunities are created by using your Work I.Q. to earn as much money as possible and then by applying your Money I.Q. in your spending, saving and investing behavior. You will learn more about growing your lifetime money supply later in this guide.

Before considering PAW and MAW growth opportunities and potential, it is important to understand money decay. Important because the factors that cause money decay are always present.

Money Decay

Since money is a commodity, like all commodities its value can be affected over time by a variety of decaying factors. On the Money Ride, your ability to minimize, neutralize or eliminate the exposure to the decaying factors will be a valuable wealth-building skill.

Consider for example, another commodity—corn. What happens if corn crop is left in the field exposed to the forces of nature? It will of course, wither and decay or be consumed by pests. However, if the corn is properly harvested, carefully stored and efficiently processed, it can be used to produce a variety of products from food to fuel.

So, what are the factors that will cause the amount and value of your PAW and MAW dollars to decay and how do they work?

There are two levels of decay which occur. The first level is the decrease in the purchasing value of each individual dollar in your money supply. This first level of decay is caused by inflation.

Inflation is essentially the dilution of the economy's money supply caused by the government increasing the number of dollars in circulation. When the number of dollars in circulation increases, the purchasing value of each dollar decreases—a dollar won't buy as much as it used to. This is due to the fact that there are more dollars available to spend relative to the number of goods available to buy.

The second level of decay is the decrease in the amount of dollars you have available—the purchasing value of your total money supply. This second level of decay is caused by three basic forces: taxes, fluctuating financial markets and spending.

Each of these second level factors can reduce your money supply in two ways. First, they reduce the total amount of Today Dollars you have. Second, you also miss out on the Tomorrow Dollars that your lost Today Dollars might have become.

Taxes are essentially the transaction fees you are obligated to pay as a citizen. There are five different types of taxes that your PAW and MAW dollars could be exposed to on the Money Ride: income taxes, property taxes, sales taxes, capital gains taxes and gift & estate taxes.

You'll pay income taxes as a percentage of the income you earn. You'll pay a sales tax as a percentage of the price of certain goods and services you buy. You'll pay a property tax on the value of real estate you own. You'll pay a capital gains tax as a percentage of the gain you earn when you sell an investment for a profit. Finally, you may have to pay a gift & estate tax on assets that you transfer to your family during your lifetime and at your death.

Because taxes are part of so many transactions, it is always important to consider the potential tax impact on your money supply in every important financial decision. In some cases you will not be able to avoid paying a tax. However, in many cases, you can manage your tax exposure by planning the timing, amount or way in which you earn, spend and invest. In these cases, when it comes to taxes, ignorance of the rules can cost you money by unknowingly paying more in taxes than the law requires you to pay.

 Passenger Tips & Tools #6

Be Smart About Your Taxes

It's important to know when you might be obligated to pay taxes, but you don't have to become an expert to be "tax smart."

In the early stage of your turn on the Money Ride, your financial situation will likely be simple enough that you can prepare your own income tax return. There are many free or inexpensive internet resources for this level of "do it yourself" tax planning.

But as your earnings increase and you begin to acquire assets, your tax situation will become more complicated. This is when being "smart" often means getting help from a tax expert. The fee you pay for an expert's advice will be worth the money you save by avoiding unnecessary taxes.

Fluctuating financial markets can cause the value of your assets to decrease in value. Periodic changes in market value are normal and they usually are associated with changes in the overall economy. The key is to understand that you have no control over market fluctuations. You must therefore consider their potential impact when deciding where and how to put your MAW dollars to work.

The decay caused by spending involves two basic types of expenses: lifestyle and financial emergencies. Lifestyle spending covers housing, food, clothes, transportation and everything else you need to live. Emergencies are what they sound like—unexpected events that cost an unpredictable amount.

All lifestyle spending naturally reduces your money supply, but the most destructive form of lifestyle spending is Stupid Spending ($-S^2$). Stupid Spending includes buying something you can't afford, paying too much or buying solely on impulse. The kind of Money Person you are and your money behavior will determine the amount of dollar decay that occurs due to lifestyle maintenance, especially when it comes to $-S^2$.

Financial emergencies will happen and you must allow for them in your planning by setting aside money in savings. If you don't, emergency expenses could seriously derail your pursuit of financial success on the Money Ride.

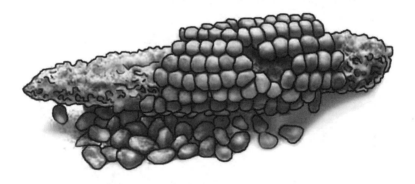

It's almost time! The roar of the roller coaster is deafening now, and as you catch a glimpse inside, you see that there is money swirling everywhere.

Time for one last quick check of what's been covered so far in your passenger's guide. You're clear on the Grabbing Rules— check. You've explored the Uses of Money and have an idea of what kind of Money Person you are—check. And you know your Money Rules backwards and forwards—check!

So, what's next? Well, you're probably beginning to realize that once your turn begins, you're going to be grabbing all these dollars and you're going to need a system for stashing and growing them. Read on, because the next section of your guide addresses this important challenge.

 Passenger Tips & Tools #7

Money Respect

Good stewardship of money starts with an enduring, fundamental respect for money—not the love of money.

Some people think that a dollar is just a piece of paper, but it actually represents a piece of a person's life measured in units of EFFORT, SACRIFICE and OPPORTUNITY. People who are careless with money too easily forget the effort and sacrifice required to find a job and make an honest living and the opportunity embedded in every dollar to build financial security and prosperity, as well as the opportunity to help others in need.

4. Stashing Your Cash

The Opportunity Vest

Regardless of whether you will be using just your hands or the biggest of nets to do your grabbing, you will need somewhere to store all the Money Ride dollars that you will be collecting. You are going to need something a lot bigger than your pockets, wallet or purse to do the job.

No problem—every passenger on the Money Ride gets their very own custom-fitted Opportunity Vest which features specially-designed pockets for storing and deploying your PAW and MAW dollars.

Your Opportunity Vest is where your work I.Q. and Money I.Q. combine to create the money flowing in, through and out of your personal economy. Money flowing into your vest from income (PAW) and out of your vest to expenses is your *cash flow—cash inflow and cash outflow*. Money that stays in your vest as cash or

savings is your *money supply*. Money that stays in your vest as investments or property is called your *equity*.

The vest has three pockets on the front and two large pockets which cover the entire back of the vest. The three front pockets are labeled "SPEND," "SAVE" and "INVEST." The back pockets are labeled "PROTECT" and "BORROW." The vest pockets represent the five domains of your money behavior. Every financial decision you make in your life will occur in the pockets on your vest. The pockets combine to form your *personal economy*. The vest pockets are elastic and will expand and shrink with your money supply based upon the money decisions you make with each dollar.

In addition to being expandable, each of your vest pockets serves a particular use of money. However, regardless of their specific use, all of the pockets operate according to the rules and dynamics of money explained earlier in this guide.

Because the pockets all operate according to the same money fundamentals, there is a dynamic connection between them. Remember the ripple effect? Based upon the law of scarcity, what you do with a dollar in one pocket has the potential to affect the dollars in your other pockets.

Vest Dynamics

Your Opportunity Vest helps you with three important jobs: 1. Organizing your financial life; 2. Maintaining a stable money supply by managing cash flow; and 3. building wealth through investments.

The vest pockets make it possible to organize your money supply according to the intended use for each dollar. This organization will help you avoid two common and related financial behavior pitfalls which can jeopardize your financial success.

The first behavior pitfall is mentally spending money you have not yet received. The second pitfall is mistakenly planning more than one use for the same dollar.

Allocating portions of your money supply in a particular pocket according to a specific use will enable you to better utilize each dollar. This efficient use of your money is especially important because your lifetime money supply is limited as described by the scarcity of money principle.

The number of dollars in each of the pockets will always be the combined product of your money behavior and the dynamics which grow and decay the value of your money. The combination will create money activity throughout your vest pockets.

The money activity throughout your Opportunity Vest happens in two stages. The first stage is using your Work I.Q. to grab and stash as many PAW dollars as possible. The second stage is using your Money I.Q. to efficiently deploy dollars in the various pockets to manage cash flow and build wealth.

As long as you are efficient with your grabbing and stashing, you will always have pockets of money to deal with whatever opportunities and challenges come your way on the Money Ride.

The remaining sections of this guide will cover in detail the purpose and dynamics of each vest pocket. You will also find examples of how fellow passengers deal with the same financial issues and concerns that you will be facing. You'll then be able to reflect on these examples as you watch how people around you on the ride are behaving with their money.

The line is moving faster now—on to the SPEND pocket!

 Passenger Tips & Tools #8

The Gravity of Money

Money has a way of behaving like the planets. It's as though every dollar in your vest has a gravitational pull on dollars outside your vest. The more dollars accumulated in a vest, the more pull. On the Money Ride you can witness the gravity of money as money leaves the vest of people who don't manage their money and gravitates to the vest of people who do.

5. The Spend Pocket

PAW at Work

The SPEND pocket is the required and automatic first stop for every PAW dollar of income you earn on the Money Ride. Decisions you make with your PAW dollars in this pocket are vital to your financial well-being and success—today and tomorrow.

The primary function of the SPEND pocket on your vest is managing cash flow to generate MAW dollars. Cash inflow from your income and cash outflow to your expenses are processed through the SPEND pocket. The process starts with a simple yet powerful question you answer with your actions every time a dollar passes through your hands—*to spend or not to spend*, that is the question!

Think before you answer, and remember that the primary objective every month is to *spend less than your earn*. Your chance for financial success starts with you making spending decisions with a purpose or plan rather than like an unconscious reflex. There are Money Ride passengers who don't realize the difference between conscious and unconscious spending and it makes them vulnerable to the temptation of stupid spending ($-S^2$). They lose control of their money, spinning their wheels and end up going nowhere financially—control your money or it will control you!

Every PAW dollar you don't spend can be converted to a MAW dollar for saving and investing. This conversion potential is the real power of PAW and it is unlocked with smart spending ($+S^2$). Using $+S^2$ to process your PAW cash flow to create MAW dollars is how you to make the important transition with your money from PAW dollars to MAW dollars. On the Money Ride this is called "bridging the gap between PAW and MAW."

Imagine two cliffs labeled "PAW" and "MAW" separated by

a bottomless chasm. It is called the "Chasm of Financial Despair" and it's filled with financial mistakes, bad habits and missed opportunities. Your challenge is to build and maintain a bridge across the chasm—a "Wealth Bridge" to get you from PAW to MAW. It's an exciting and harrowing task, but you won't have to go it alone because you'll have help.

Your Friend Bud

Meet Bud, the friendly Money Ride attendant. When it comes to building your wealth bridge from PAW to MAW—do not fear because Bud is here! Bud will help you get from PAW to MAW— Bud-get! That's right, your wealth bridge from PAW to MAW is called a "budget."

Your monthly budget will help you become financially self-reliant by helping you manage cash flow to pay for two basic aspects of your life: (1.) lifestyle; and (2.) life goals. Lifestyle expenses comprise every dollar you spend on living. Lifestyle expenses include, but are not limited to, food, housing, car, insurance and entertainment. Life goal expenses comprise every dollar you will need to reach future goals. Life goals include but are not limited to education, vacations, retirement, and buying a new car or home.

Managing your cash flow to balance lifestyle and life goals by spending less than your earn produces excess PAW dollars which you can spend, save or invest. If you save or invest the excess PAW dollars, they convert to MAW dollars which can be used in your SAVE and INVEST pockets. If you spend the excess PAW dollars, they leave your Opportunity Vest and gravitate to the vests of others. A monthly budget will help you prevent your money from needlessly leaving your vest by keeping track of your spending behavior.

Budget = D²

There are a number of different ways to design a budget. The most important thing to remember about your budget is that your behavior is more critical than the design. There is a very simple Money Ride formula to help you remember this important point:

$$\text{BUDGET} = \text{DISCRETION} \times \text{DISCIPLINE}$$

Discretion is the thought you put into making your "to spend or not to spend" choices and decisions. Discipline is sticking to the monthly budgeting process based on your goals and objectives. Discretion and discipline are the foundation of your budget because these two D's enable you to control your money.

Building Your Budget

The basic function of a monthly budget is tracking your cash inflow from income and your cash outflow to expenses, savings and investments. A budget consists of a list of your income and expenses derived from all of your earning and spending data. You will need a system to keep track of all your money activity so that your budget is accurate. A budget system does not have to be complicated, but it should include a procedure and tools for collecting, recording, evaluating and storing all of your transaction data. Each of the tools corresponds to a step in your budgeting procedure, making it easier to establish budgeting as a sound money behavior.

The first tool you will need to create is a data-collecting tool used to save the "source document" from each of your monthly transactions. Your source documents include paycheck stubs, cash receipts, credit receipts and bank slips. This means that every time you earn, spend, borrow, deposit or withdraw money, you save the piece of paper generated by the transaction.

You will need a device where you can stash your source documents from each day when you get home. One idea is to use a piece of wood with a protruding nail, but you can also use an envelope, or large paper clip. It is, however best to able to separate your documents into three transaction types: "cash," "credit" and "bank." You can use a single holder or create one holder for each transaction type. You document holder should be visible and accessible as a habit-building reminder—like your very own Jiminy Cricket budgeting device.

In addition to your collecting tool you will need a tool for

Spending a Dollar

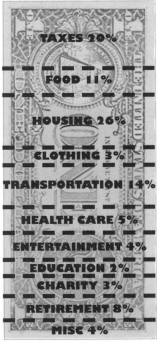

Passenger Tips & Tools #9

Are You S.M.A.R.T. About Your Goals?

1. Write a description of what it is you want as though you already have it. Be **Specific** about what it is and how it feels to know you have accomplished it.
2. List the steps you will need to take to achieve your goal. The steps must be **Measurable** so that you can track your progress...how much...how many, etc.
3. Develop a "can do" attitude about achieving your goal... know that you are deserving of what it is you want and be confident that your goal is **Attainable**.
4. Be **Realistic** about your goal. Be clear that it is something that you are both determined and able to accomplish. Aim high and be real.
5. Give yourself a deadline for achieving your goal so that it is **Timely** in terms of your current situation.

recording and evaluating your data. Your tool for this part of your system is called a "budget worksheet." Your worksheet is simply a list of all of you income and expenses. Expenses should be divided into four main categories: (1) Needs-fixed; (2) Needs-variable (3) Wants-fixed; and (4) Wants-variable. Needs are things that you must have to live, like food, housing and clothing. Wants are everything else, including amounts to be set aside in savings and investments for future goals. Fixed expenses cost the same amount every month, like rent or loan payments. Variable expenses cost an

amount based on how much you use, like food, utilities and enter-tainment. You can simply list the various categories or divide them into four sections.

One expense item deserves special mention: expense reserves. Expense reserves are used to pay expenses that instead of monthly, are paid periodically: quarterly (every 90 days), semi-annually (every 180 days); or annually. The total future amount to be paid is converted to a monthly expense amount. The monthly amount is treated as a fixed expense and transferred to the expense reserve account each month. By setting aside a smaller amount in the months prior to the payment due date, the money is available when it is needed. Remember to use the expense reserve account for paying periodic expenses.

In addition to organizing and recording data, a budget work-sheet is used to evaluate spending behavior, goal progress and over-all financial health. Additionally, categorizing expenses into needs, wants, fixed and variable helps you be more objective about evaluat-ing adjustments to your spending.

Once you have your document holder and worksheet complet-ed you need to create a tool for storing your monthly budget docu-ments and worksheet. For this you can use either a large envelope or a file folder. Whichever you use, on the outside cover label across the top headings: "Month," "Income," "Expenses" and "Net +/–". You also will need an envelope labeled with month and year for saving all of your receipts, bank slips, etc.

Your Budget System in Action

The steps that follow describe a manual budget system. Computer software, smart phone applications and websites are convenient and useful for organizing and analyzing financial data. However, track-ing your money activity by hand will help you develop the disci-pline needed to make budgeting a habit. Doing it by hand trains your brain and training your brain is vital to building sound money habits.

Remember the formula, Budget=D^2 The success of your BUD-

 Passenger Tips & Tools #10

Managing Your Bank Accounts

Managing your bank accounts is part of the budgeting process. In order for a budget to work, you must always know accurately how much cash is available in your bank account—your "bank balance."

To know how much money you have in the bank, you must compare and adjust your own bank balance record with the bank's monthly statement to make sure that all old and new transactions are included in both. This is called a bank reconciliation report and it is used to *balance* a bank account. You can do it by hand or use a computer software program to balance your bank account and create a bank reconciliation report. Regardless of how you do it, managing your bank accounts is vital to the function and reliability of your budget.

GET will EQUAL your ability to exercise DISCRETION in your spending choices and your ability to develop the DISCIPLINE to stick with the system. Try to follow the system as it is described for at least three months. This will be enough time for you to experience the positive difference a budget can make.

After three months, you can tweak the design and steps to suit you, or switch to a different approach. Regardless of which system you use, the most important thing is that budgeting becomes a lifetime habit.

Here are the budgeting steps:

1. Place your document collector in a high traffic area such as the kitchen counter, bedroom dresser, etc., where you will see it every day as you come and go.

2. Save every source document from *every transaction* you do, no matter how small the transaction amount. Keep every credit and cash receipt, ATM and bank deposit slips and paycheck

stubs—every piece of paper for every dollar earned, saved, spent or invested. Place your source documents on/in your document collection tool by transaction type:

   a. CASH nail: Receipts from transactions where you paid with cash, check, debit card, prepaid credit card, gift card or any other cash equivalent.

   b. CREDIT nail: Receipts from transactions where you paid with a credit card, or any form of loan.

   c. BANK nail: Deposit and withdrawal receipts and ATM slips, but not checks.

For any transaction where you do not receive a source document, create one using a small piece of paper listing the amount and type (cash/credit/bank) . Additionally, if it is not obvious from the source, it will be helpful if you note on each document the specific category for a transaction such as "food", "car" or "gift".

3. At the end of the month, using your monthly budget sheet:

   a. Take the receipts from your Budget Board and list the category and amount for each source document in the appropriate quadrant on your budget sheet.

JUNE 2015: TOTAL INCOME: $3500
TOTAL EXPENSES: $2560
NET +/- : $ 940 +SAVINGS/-SAVINGS

1. NEEDS-FIXED	3. WANTS-FIXED
RENT $800.	CABLE TV: $50.
CAR INS. $120.	GYM: $30.
HEALTH INS. $200.	
	#3 TOTAL: $80
#1 TOTAL: $1,120.	

2. NEEDS-VARIABLE	4. WANTS-VARIABLE
FOOD $400.	ENTERTAINMENT $210.
GAS & ELEC. $110.	CELL/DATA $ 35.
CELL/BASE $ 30.	CLOTHES $100.
CLOTHES $ 50.	
CAR GAS/OIL $250.	
PERSONAL CARE $ 75.	
MISC. $100.	#4 TOTAL: $345.
#2 TOTAL: $1,015.	TOTAL WANTS: $425.
TOT. NEEDS: $2,135.	

b. Calculate the total for items in each quadrant and enter total at the bottom of the section. Calculate the total for the two NEEDS quadrants and enter at the bottom left of the form. Calculate the total for the two WANTS quadrants and enter at the bottom right of the sheet.

c. Enter your total income for the month at the top of the form at TOTAL INCOME.

d. Calculate the total for NEEDS plus WANTS from the bottom of the form and enter the total on the second line at the top of the form at TOTAL EXPENSES"

e. Subtract TOTAL EXPENSES from TOTAL INCOME and enter result on the third line titled "NET +/–" at the top of the sheet .

4. Using your Budget Folder:

a. Enter the amounts for TOTAL INCOME, TOTAL EXPENSES and NET in the appropriate columns on the outside of the folder.

b. Put all of your source documents in the monthly receipts envelope and place the envelope and your monthly budget form in the folder and file it.

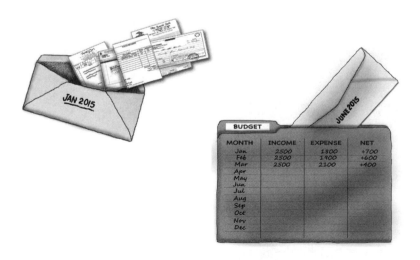

CONGRATULATIONS! You have now completed your first monthly budget cycle and taken your first big step towards financial self-reliance! You can now continue to use the system comparing your money behavior from month to month. This structure and process will enable you to stay on track toward reaching your financial goals.

Use your budget to efficiently deploy your PAW dollars to balance your spending between lifestyle and life goals.

You then will be able to use this information to make adjustments to your budget to improve the PAW-to-MAW efficiency in your SPEND pocket. This flexibility to make budget adjustments as things change in your life is important to maintaining your lifestyle and pursuing your life goals.

Your budget will serve as your structured, yet flexible spending plan, based upon discretion and discipline. It will help you to use the power of "spend less than you earn" to generate a continuous cash flow of MAW dollars for building wealth.

Now it's time to reap the rewards of the sound money habit of smart spending $(+S^2)$—on to the SAVE pocket!

Passenger Watch

D^2 Anyone?

All the Suzie's and Freddy's on the Money Ride love their SPEND pocket!

Suzie lives to spend and at the rate she burns through money, she will never see the MAW side of the chasm…but sadly she doesn't yet realize that her overspending will lead to nowhere for lack of a wealth bridge.

Freddy, yes, he definitely knows how to spend money, but unlike Suzie he is aware of his limits—most of the time. He has to be careful to avoid the temptation of always needing the latest and greatest gizmo or gadget.

There are also some Freddys on the ride who really can't afford to be a Freddy, but they love showing off. They will find out later the true cost of pretending.

Sonya and Franklin always keep their D^2 well focused in the SPEND pocket.

Sonya always has another investment in mind and wants to spend as little as possible to leave more for investing.

Franklin is the king of budgeting. He keeps careful track of every penny. But he gets carried away with penny pinching at times and forgets to take time to treat himself to some fun.

6. The Save Pocket

Here Comes MAW

The SAVE pocket is the first stop for the MAW dollars created by smart spending ($+S^2$) in your SPEND pocket. These MAW dollars are your reward for sticking to your budget.

Once your MAW dollars are safely across the chasm, they serve their first two important purposes in your SAVE pocket.

The first purpose is to provide a lifestyle safety net for unexpected expenses. These MAW dollars are called "emergency reserves."

Emergency reserves differ from expense reserves. Expense reserves are stored in a checking account to pay upcoming expenses, but emergency reserves are stored in a savings account and used to pay unexpected living expenses.

The second purpose is funding short-term financial goals. These are goals with a duration of four years or less. The MAW dollars used to fund them are simply called "savings."

Once you have fully funded these two purposes, any of your additional MAW dollars can be put to work in the INVEST pocket.

Save = Safe

This is the basic SAVE pocket formula, and like the budget formula from the SPEND pocket, it is obviously not math. Since the money in your SAVE pocket is intended to establish your safe foothold, it is called "safe money."

Safe money is essentially what its name suggests, but it has three aspects to its definition—location, risk and liquidity.

Location has two dimensions: (1) institution—the financial institution where you deposit your MAW money; and (2) account—a record of how much you have deposited with the institution.

On the Money Ride, institution means "bank." Banks, credit unions and savings & loans are all considered banks.

Think of an "account" as your personal bag of money at the bank. The bank calls the money in your savings account your "principal." There are different types of bags with different features. You will be able to choose, according to your saving objective, which type of bag(s) you use to store the money in your account.

Risk is the chance that you may lose money. A loss can result from downward fluctuations in the economy, financial markets or the value of a specific account. In the SAVE pocket, risk is to be avoided at all times. You will learn later in this section about how your SAVE pocket money can be protected from risk.

Liquidity is the ease with which your MAW money principal can be converted to cash on demand. Liquidity is an important consideration with every SAVE pocket account you establish. You want to be able to get cash when you need it.

The "Save = Safe" formula is a reminder, telling you to look for safety and liquidity when you stash your MAW dollars in your SAVE pocket. Just remember that with every MAW dollar in your SAVE pocket, safety is the first requirement.

As with every pocket on your Opportunity Vest, the dollars you stash in your SAVE pocket will require you to choose and decide. There are three basic questions you will have to answer with the MAW dollars you'll be vesting in your SAVE pocket:

1. How much?
2. How soon/How long?
3. Where?

These questions are interdependent, and the answers will change with your circumstances as you travel along on the Money Ride.

How Much?

"How much?" is the first and most important question you must answer with your MAW dollars in the SAVE pocket. Because it is the most important question, it is sometimes also the most challenging. This is because "How much?" must also take into account "How soon/How long?" your SAVE pocket dollars may be needed.

In order to form sound money habits in your SAVE pocket, it is important to treat saving each month as though it were an expense. This means designating an amount for savings in your budget each month to maintain a flow of MAW dollars for saving and investing.

The amount you choose as your SAVE pocket target will depend upon the amount of PAW money you grab, the cost of your lifestyle and the anticipated cost of fulfilling your goals.

A good first target for lifestyle reserves would be an amount equal to your total living expenses for one month. The next reserves target would be three months' expenses. Your final reserves target would be six to twelve months' expenses.

As an example, let's say that you allocate at least 10% each month of your PAW dollars to your "MAW dollar expense." After ten months of budgeting you would then have the equivalent of one month's total income stashed in your SAVE pocket.

Once you have figured out the reserves amount, you'll then decide how much money you need for goals. While you will have short-term and long-term goals, only money for short-term goals is stashed in the SAVE pocket. You will learn about stashing money for long-term goals later in the INVEST pocket.

 Passenger Tips & Tools #11

What's Your Savings Target?

Think of savings as paying yourself first...setting money aside for you before you spend your first dollar each month.

What percentage of your take-home pay should you save each month? 10% is a good beginning target amount for establishing a sound money habit of saving.

But if you want to stay ahead of taxes, inflation and the other economic factors that can cause your money supply to decay, 20% of take-home pay should be your savings goal.

The price and the completion schedule for each goal will dictate total the amount you will need to have vested in your SAVE pocket.

Each short-term goal has its own cost and importance determined by your life priorities. First you will have to determine the amount of money needed for each goal. Then the challenge will be to maintain a consistent flow of MAW dollars into the SAVE pocket to fund each goal.

Your target amount for all short-term goals should be part of your MAW dollars expense in your monthly budget. This will ensure that sufficient PAW dollars are converted to MAW dollars every month to cover the cost of your short-term goals.

Now that you know how to answer the "How much?" question, you're ready to move on to the next SAVE pocket question: "How soon/How long?"

 Passenger Tips & Tools #12

How Liquid Is Your Savings Account?

Basic Savings & Money Market—You can withdraw cash from your account on demand anytime with no penalty or fee if you withdraw money early.

Certificate of Deposit—Has a specified minimum holding time (e.g. 30 days – 2 years) during which you must keep your money on deposit. If you withdraw cash early, you forfeit interest you would have earned if you had waited until the maturity date.

How Soon/How Long?

After "How much?" comes the "How soon/How long?" question. The first part of the question deals with the liquid aspect of your SAVE pocket money: How soon do you need it, and how quickly can it be converted to cash?

How soon might you need to rely on your SAVE pocket reserves to help you through a financial emergency or take advantage of a financial opportunity? The timing is as impossible to predict as the amount, which makes having liquid dollars so essential.

This is why it is so important to start stashing dollars in your SAVE pocket as soon and as regularly as possible.

Now that you realize that you might need to depend on your savings at any moment, the next question is how long might you need to rely on your savings to supplement your sole monthly income?

What if you wanted to take advantage of a life opportunity which required that you move to a different city, state or country? How much would it cost to relocate, start your new life and live until your first paycheck arrives?

What about emergencies? What if because of an illness or injury you couldn't work for a while? How many months of living expenses might you need until you recover?

Finally, what about your life goals, like education, buying a home or a car, starting a new job or changing careers? These represent a potential need for MAW dollars to satisfy a short-term goal.

Regardless of the need or timing, the "How soon/How long?" question helps determine the savings goal and the deposits needed to reach it.

Now on to the last SAVE pocket question—"Where?"

Where?

The best place to put the MAW dollars you stash in your SAVE pocket is in a bank.

Banks may differ in name or type, but they all perform three basic functions—storing money, processing money and lending money. They provide storing and lending services by taking in deposits from customers and making loans to customers. Banks are authorized to lend a specified amount of money, which is based on the value of the bank's total deposits. Banks thus need deposits to make loans.

Banks attract deposits by offering you a fee to store your MAW dollars there. This fee is called "interest" and it is measured in percentages called "interest rates." The bank pays you interest based on your *principal.* Principal is the amount of money you have in a savings account.

 Passenger Tips & Tools #13

How Safe Is Your Money?

All banks offer deposit accounts where the safety of your money is guaranteed by the government through the Federal Deposit Insurance Corporation (FDIC). The FDIC guarantees the safety of a passenger's account up to $250,000 per bank.

One way banks earn a profit is by charging borrowing customers an interest rate for loans that is higher than the interest rate they pay savings customers on their deposits. So, you receive interest income and the bank earns a profit creating loans to circulate money throughout the economy.

The longer you agree to leave your money in an account with a bank, the higher interest rate you should expect to be paid. This is the basic contract or deal you make with a bank when you give it your MAW dollars for safekeeping.

Since the interest your money earns is your incentive to store money at a bank, it is important to understand how interest works.

Interest is typically calculated using a special type of math formula called "compounding." With compounding, the financial institution pays you interest on your principal for the period of time they store your money. The interest you earn each period is added to your account value.

The rate of interest you earn is expressed as an annual rate. The yearly rate is then divided into 365 daily interest increments. For each day your money is stored, you earn $\frac{1}{365}$ of the annual interest.

The advantage of compounding is that you not only earn interest on your principal, you also earn interest on the interest

Passenger Tips & Tools #14

Compounding Formula:
$$FV = P(1+i)^n$$

The compounding formula is also known as the "Time Value of Money Formula." It is the only Money Ride formula that is based on actual math.

FV = Future value
P = Present value/principal
i = Interest rate
n = Number of time periods

Using this formula, if you deposited $100 PAW dollars in a savings account at 5% interest for ten years, your MAW dollars in the account would grow to $162.89.

you earned in prior periods—this is compounding in action. Compounding is the ripple effect of saving, and this is why your SAVE pocket money qualifies as MAW, "Money at Work."

 Passenger Tips & Tools #15

The Rule of 72

If you want to know how long it will take for compounding to double the value of your PAW dollars, divide "72" by the interest rate your money will earn.

Example: If the bank offers to pay you 7.2% interest annually on your principal, it will take how many years for your money to double in value?
$$72 \div 7.2 = 10$$

It will take ten years for your principal to double if you earn 7.2% interest each year.

In addition to compounding, there is a second type of interest formula that you should be aware of, called "simple interest." This type of interest is rarely used, but it deserves mention so that you are able to make smart SAVE pocket money decisions if you are offered this option.

Simple interest is, as its name suggests, simple. Unlike compounding, simple interest is paid each period on the principal only. There is no interest paid on the interest received in prior periods.

While compound and simple interest produce different results, they share a common dynamic—the higher the interest rate, the faster your MAW dollars grow each year.

Interest rates are important, but they are not the only factor to consider in selecting a financial institution. Another important consideration is the type of account in which you choose to store your SAVE pocket money.

 Passenger Tips & Tools #16

Simple Interest Formula:

FV = P + (P x i x n)

From the prior example you know that $100 will grow to $162.89 in ten years at 5% using compounding.

If you use the simple interest formula to calculate the interest earned, you would end up with $150.00 after ten years.

The longer the period or higher the interest, the greater the difference in ending value would be.

There will be many different types of savings programs to choose from, such as money market accounts, savings accounts, treasury bills and certificates of deposit. The "How soon/How long?" question will influence your choice because these accounts store money for different lengths of time. Your choice will mean matching your short-term and long-term savings goals with an appropriately timed savings account.

The process of matching your savings goals to the specific type of account is called "staging." Staging involves positioning your MAW dollars in an order that reflects when you will need a particular amount of your SAVE dollars for a particular purpose.

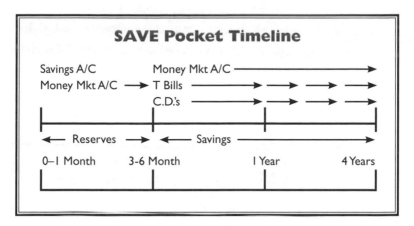

Think of this staging visually as a timeline of MAW money in your SAVE pocket that matches your timeline of cash needs. Accounts designated for reserves would be at the left end of the timeline. Those designated for savings would be located along the timeline in the diagram from left (short term) to right (long term).

Accounts for storing reserves and short-term savings would be those positioned on the left in savings accounts or money market accounts. Savings account money for life goals from one to four years in the future, would be positioned from left to right on the timeline in treasury bills and certificates of deposit. This approach ensures that an adequate amount of SAVE money is always available when it is needed for emergencies, short-term goals and opportunities.

It is important to realize that, excluding deposits, not much wealth building will take place in your SAVE pocket because of the relationship between time and money. The MAW dollars stored in your SAVE pocket will be there for a limited amount of time. Since interest earned is the product of principal, the rate and the number of periods it is earned. SAVE pocket dollars usually don't generate a lot of interest earnings because the interest rate is typically too low and earnings period too short to take full advantage of long-term compound interest.

Real wealth-building, based on time and money, happens in your INVEST pocket, where you will learn to work with larger amounts of MAW dollars over longer periods of time.

So, the sooner you stash the appropriate amount of MAW dollars in your SAVE pocket, the sooner you can move on to the challenges, excitement and rewards waiting for you in the INVEST pocket.

No time to waste—on to the INVEST pocket!

 Passenger Watch

Is It Worth Saving?

Suzie naturally struggles with saving because she spends all and sometimes more than she earns every month. Her only incentive for saving is her next big purchase.

Sonya loves investing and because she understands risk, she knows how important reserves are. Sonya accumulated her six month reserves in less than a year so that she could start investing as soon as possible.

Franklin's saving habits are much like Sonya's but his motives are more about safety and stability than maximizing his investment opportunities. He carefully tracks his savings percentage each month and is very careful about where and how he stashes his savings.

Freddy is actually very good at saving because he knows his savings are his safety net for maintaining his lifestyle and image.

7. The Invest Pocket

MAW Goes to Work

The INVEST pocket is where your ability to create MAW dollars through the efficient use of money in your SPEND pocket is rewarded. This is where your MAW dollars apply their real wealth-building muscle.

Once you begin stashing MAW dollars in your INVEST pocket, the focus of your Money I.Q. shifts from smart spending and saving to making the most of investment opportunities to build wealth.

 Passenger Tips & Tools #17

Successful Investing Takes a Lot of D^2

Before you invest, remember how hard you had to work to grab your PAW dollars and how much D^2 it took to create your first MAW dollars.

You will need an equal amount of discretion and discipline to design an effective investment strategy and stay with it for the long run. So, respect your MAW dollars for the hard work and D^2 they represent by always being vigilant and diligent in managing your investments.

The opportunities will be many and varied, and your financial success will depend on your ability to make informed choices. This means you need to know *what* you are doing, *how* it works and *where* it fits in relation to your other financial goals and objectives.

Before we get into the specifics of how the INVEST pocket works, it's important that you have an understanding about the INVEST pocket's fundamental purpose: wealth—what it is and what it means to you.

Wealth

On the Money Ride there are two kinds of wealth: Financial Wealth and Personal Wealth.

Financial wealth is the market value of assets and the income generated by assets. The income provides cash flow to live on. The market value provides an asset's current price and its potential for future growth. Financial wealth is money at work (MAW) in your INVEST pocket. The MAW dollars are invested to grow asset value and to generate income. So, MAW has the potential to produce not just Tomorrow Dollars and Today Dollars.

When you retire and you're no longer grabbing PAW dollars, your wealth assets must generate MAW income to replace the PAW income. Your MAW income is generated directly by an asset such as rental income, interest income, stock dividends etc. This MAW income is called "passive income" because you don't have to actively grab these dollars as you do with PAW dollars. Passive income is the Today Dollar value of your INVEST pocket dollars.

In addition to the MAW income, the potential future increase in the market value of your wealth assets offers the potential for increased future income. This increase in future value and income

---

 Passenger Tips & Tools #18

The Tomorrow Dollar Value of Your Money

Every Today Dollar, represented by PAW and MAW dollars in your money supply has the potential to grow if you hang on to it and efficiently put it to work. This is the Tomorrow Dollar value of your money—it's potential to build wealth in the form of assets which generate income and/or grow in value.

Remember…attitudes and values about wealth are personal, but the money rules and mechanics for building wealth are the same for everyone.

The primary challenge of building wealth is balancing your consumption of Today Dollars with the need to create a supply of Tomorrow Dollars.

helps insulate your wealth and cash flow against the eroding effects of inflation, taxes and expenses. The potential to generate future income is the Tomorrow Dollar value of the wealth you create with your INVEST pocket dollars.

On the Money Ride, the whole point of pursuing financial success and wealth is to live a happier, more fulfilled life. This makes your definition of personal wealth as important as your definition of financial wealth.

Personal wealth includes aspects of your life where it is not money itself that is important, but rather the abundance of people, experiences and opportunities that you enjoy. These may include values like supporting a family, reaching personal goals and helping others in need.

Your personal definition influences the lifestyle you *want* to live, which in turn determines the amount of money you'll *need* to live.

Your working definition of wealth will help you focus on your INVEST pocket goals and monitor your wealth-building progress.

There are four dynamics at work in the INVEST pocket which make it very different from the SAVE pocket: risk, reward, growth and income. These are the roller coaster "ups and downs" of building wealth.

Invest = Risk

You'll remember that the primary characteristic of the MAW dollars stashed in your SAVE pocket is that they are safe dollars (SAVE = Safe). This means that there is little or no danger in the SAVE pocket of losing your original MAW dollars.

In the INVEST pocket there is always risk—the possibility that you may lose some or all of the MAW dollars you stash there. This is what makes INVEST pocket dollars fundamentally different from SAVE pocket dollars, which are exposed to little or no risk.

In order to successfully deal with risk, you must start by asking yourself two basic questions:

1. What is the type and degree of risk?
2. What is my risk tolerance?

Answering these two questions involves some "figuring" and some "feeling."

The figuring part is doing your homework to determine what risks are present in a potential investment and how much risk you can afford to take. This will involve identifying the source of risk, how it might occur, how it might be offset or avoided and ultimately how much money it may cause you to lose. This research is an important aspect of your Money I.Q.

The feeling part is being honest with yourself about how the thought of losing your MAW dollars makes you feel. This is called your risk tolerance, and it is based upon how risk affects you emotionally and financially.

Figuring and feeling are both part of every investment decision you will make on the Money Ride. So, let's explore the figuring first, then we'll talk about the feeling part of the process.

What makes risk so interesting and challenging is that there are different types or elements of risk in every investment opportunity.

There are three basic types or levels of risk which you should be aware of. Each represents a chance to make or lose precious MAW dollars, so pay attention to these when considering every investment opportunity.

The Three Levels of Risk
1. The Economy
This is the "big picture" level of risk. Both the general state of the economy and the major economic factors of interest rates, inflation and financial markets can have an impact on the performance of investments.

Generally, the performance of investments will reflect the performance of the overall economy. Interest rates, inflation rates and the financial markets serve as indicators of the health and direction of the economy and have their own particular impact on investment performance.

2. The Industry

The next level of risk research involves analyzing the industry in which the investment operates.

Is the investment in a profitable and stable industry?

Is it an emerging industry with a future, an established industry with a history or a fading industry offering outmoded products or services?

Is there a current demand and/or future demand for the industry's goods and services?

Is the industry reliant on consumer spending or government spending?

These are the types of questions you need to explore when assessing the potential of investing in a particular industry.

3. Investment

Once you have completed your research on the risk implications of the economy and the industry involved, your last step is to analyze the risk attributed to a specific investment. This may involve investigating a company, a real estate property or an investment company that manages MAW dollars for investors.

Is it profitable, financially strong and well managed?

Is there demand for its products or services?

Is it known in its industry for some special feature or innovation?

The best candidates may not be obvious at first, but by asking the right questions, the investments with solid wealth-building potential will be easier to identify.

You'll have to do your INVEST pocket homework to learn as much as you can about every source of risk before you invest. Remember, on the Money Ride homework is fun and profitable. Smart, disciplined passengers get paid to do their INVEST pocket homework—with wealth!

After you have done the figuring work of identifying the type and degree of risk, it's time to explore the feeling aspect of risk.

If you want to maximize the wealth potential of your INVEST pocket and enjoy life, it is important to feel comfortable with the degree of risk in your investments—remember your risk tolerance.

Your risk tolerance is influenced by the kind of Money Person you are and your understanding of how money and your investments work.

The more anxious you are about losing MAW dollars, the less tolerant of risk you will be. However, by understanding more about an investment, you can reduce your risk anxiety and be more confident and comfortable with your investment choices.

Now that you are aware of how risk influences your investment decisions, it's time for you to learn about the second unique INVEST pocket dynamic: Reward.

Invest = Reward

Your research on risk is never complete until it gives equal consideration to the dynamic of reward. Reward is the potential to make money on an investment, either from an increase in its market value (growth) or from the cash flow (income) it generates.

Risk and reward are the two sides of the investment decision coin. Since either side may result, the likelihood of each happening must be compared in order to make an informed investment decision.

You must research the potential reward of an investment offer just as thoroughly as you study its risk, so that you can gauge its probability as accurately as possible. Doing your homework on *both* sides of the investment decision coin will help you feel more comfortable with your investment choices.

Your understanding of the risk/reward relationship will help you intelligently expand your risk tolerance, regardless of what type of Money Person you are. This expanded tolerance will mean that more investment opportunities will qualify as appropriate choices for you.

 Passenger Tips & Tools #19

Risk vs. Reward

When you evaluate the risks of an investment always remember that the potential rewards of the investment must be greater than the risks by a great deal.

Invest = Growth

The overall goal of every INVEST pocket decision is to build wealth through investing. Therefore, growth is the objective with every MAW dollar you stash in your INVEST pocket. The potential for growth is what you should look for in every investment opportunity that comes your way on the Money Ride. The key to your financial success will be using your Money I.Q. to transform growth potential into real wealth.

In order to gauge your success at transforming growth potential into wealth, you first have to know how to measure growth and the wealth it produces. On the Money Ride, the wealth you create by investing MAW dollars is measured in the value of assets. An asset is defined as anything you own which has two basic characteristics: the potential to grow in value and the potential to produce income.

Any increase in an asset's market value in excess of what you originally paid for it is money gained in growth. Growth can be converted to cash by selling an investment for a profit.

The key is to invest in assets which achieve growth that is continual and consistent. This sustained growth must also be at a pace or rate sufficient to stay ahead of the factors which erode money, such as taxes, inflation, fluctuating interest rates and market declines. Only by growth outpacing these eroding factors can real wealth be created.

Another important aspect of growth you must be aware of is the element of time. The value of some investments can increase very quickly. For instance, stock share prices can change dramatically in a matter of seconds or minutes. However, growth is typically not about getting rich quickly. While there are sophisticated and aggressive investing strategies offering the potential for large short-term gains, the fundamentals of growth are based on long-term participation in an investment.

Invest = Income

In addition to growth, the second valuable characteristic of investment assets is the capacity to generate income. Income is the cash generated by an investment. Income can be in the form of a dividend as with stocks, interest as with bonds or rent as with real estate. The income objective typically takes a back seat to growth in the early stages of the wealth building process. However, as you reach the end of your PAW dollar–grabbing years, generating income from your MAW dollars will become the primary objective.

In order to meet this switch in emphasis from growth to income, you will have to reallocate a portion of your PAW dollars from assets that do not generate income to those that do. This means moving some of your MAW dollars into investments that generate interest, dividends, rents, etc.

Passenger Tips & Tools #20

Automatic Investing

Time and discipline are important in successful investing. So start early and try making your investment contributions automatic to sustain a disciplined investing program...time will take care of the rest.

Research investment opportunities which allow you to electronically transfer MAW dollars from your bank account each month to your investment accounts.

Though the primary objective for your MAW dollars may shift to generating income, you will still want to have some of your MAW dollars invested for growth so that you will have sufficient assets to generate future lifestyle income.

Next up, we will explore the mechanics of investing so that you will be better equipped to evaluate the growth and income potential of an investment before you invest.

Mechanics of Investing

There are three fundamental ways to put your MAW dollars to work in your INVEST pocket: Invest, Diversify and Reinvest. Regardless of which investments you choose for growing your MAW dollars, your decisions will involve one or more of these three key mechanics.

Invest

This is the obvious purpose of your INVEST pocket. It represents the action of regularly stashing MAW dollars in your INVEST pocket as investment capital to build wealth.

The regular, systematic stashing of MAW dollars in your INVEST pocket is a sound money habit which is vital to your financial success on the Money Ride.

Diversify

Diversification is a valuable tool for dealing with investment risk and increasing wealth-building opportunity. If you simply accumulate all of your MAW dollars in a single investment, you will always be exposed to the same type and degree of risk. You will also be limiting yourself to only one asset category to build wealth. The single investment approach can work if you are lucky, but luck is not a reliable approach to dealing with risk or building an investment portfolio. Even if you decide to invest exclusively in a particular category of investment like real estate or stocks, it will still make sense to diversify your holdings in two or more investments within the same category.

Diversifying to mange risk involves investing in two or more investments with different risk characteristics. This approach will effectively spread your exposure to risk over the different investments, rather than concentrating all of your risk exposure in a single investment. Keep in mind that diversification does not totally eliminate risk.

Diversifying to expand wealth building opportunities involves owning a variety of either different categories of assets or different assets within a single category. The value of assets is affected differently over time by various economic factors. Each individual asset or category has its own up and down business cycle of performance. Owning a variety of assets creates a greater probability that some wealth building will always be happening somewhere in your INVEST pocket.

Reinvest

Like a farmer harvesting corn, you will be harvesting your crop of new MAW dollars which grow from the seeds of your original MAW investment capital and using it as seed to grow additional wealth.

When an asset becomes worth more than what you paid for it, you have the opportunity to sell the asset to convert profit to cash for reinvesting. You will first have to pay a tax on the profit you earn from selling the asset and will then have the net after tax amount available to invest.

With some types of assets like stocks, bonds or mutual funds you can convert your profit to cash by selling just a portion of your total holdings. This allows you to leave your original investment intact and reinvest the profits which are new MAW dollars.

🐎 Passenger Tips & Tools #21

Reinvesting Your MAW Profits

If you invest $1,000 to buy 100 shares of stock for $10/share and 10 years later its market value increases to $20/share, the increase represents a profit of $1,000.

You could then sell 50 shares for $20/share, generating $1,000 in cash including $500 in profit...pay tax of approximately $100, and have $900 left to reinvest.

You would end up with your original $1,000 still invested in 50 shares and an additional $900 to reinvest in a new investment to diversify your portfolio.

Assets can also provide opportunities for reinvesting by producing new MAW dollars in the form of profits from income. This simply involves taking the income produced by an asset and using it to purchase an additional new asset. For example, I could take the dividends received from a stock, interest from a bond or the rent income from real estate and invest it to purchase more stock, bonds or real estate.

Whether from growth in market value or income, reinvesting profits builds wealth by either increasing the value or number of assets you own. Each new asset represents an additional opportunity to build wealth through growth and/or income. Intelligent reinvesting allows you to keep your MAW dollars working at optimum wealth-building capacity.

Investing wisely requires an investment strategy suited to your objectives and resources—your goals and your supply of MAW dollars. To develop your strategy, you can start by asking yourself the same three basic questions you used in the SAVE pocket: How much?, How soon/How long? and Where?

How Much?

Just as with the SAVE pocket, "How much?" is the first and most important question you must answer with your MAW dollars in the INVEST pocket…with one difference. In the INVEST pocket, "How much?" is a two-part question. The first question is, "How much do you have to invest?" The second question is, "How much do you need for a particular life goal or objective?"

The answer to the first part will be a function of how successful you are at sustaining smart spending habits and maintaining an appropriate amount of savings. Remember that maintaining control over your money supply in the SPEND and SAVE pockets produces a supply of MAW dollars for investing.

The answer to the second part involves estimating the amount of money you will need for various life goals. Once you have established a goal, you can then analyze the growth potential and risk potential of various investments to find those best suited to your goal. The analysis will indicate how much you will need to invest in order to reach your goal. Your research may lead you to selecting a single investment or multiple investments toward funding a particular goal.

The type of Money Person you are will also be a factor in your investment selections. Your tolerance of risk will be the dominant influence, both in terms of the amount you invest and the type of investment you choose. Because of the constant presence of risk, it is impossible to accurately predict the future value of an investment.

Passengers on the Money Ride who don't mind risk tend to prefer more aggressive investments. These are investments which offer the potential to either make a lot of money or lose a lot of money. They may also offer quick profits, as opposed to slow and steady long-term growth of MAW dollars.

On the other hand, passengers who aren't comfortable with risk prefer more conservative investments. These are investments where there is little risk of losing MAW dollars. They are usually less likely to make a lot of money or make it as quickly as aggressive, high-risk investments. At times, the conservative passenger may feel more comfortable keeping more MAW dollars in the SAVE pocket rather than in the INVEST pocket.

So, ultimately your success in the INVEST pocket will come down to how many MAW dollars you have to invest, how many MAW dollars you want or need for future goals and what kind of Money Person you are.

Finally, in order to maintain sound money habits for investing, it is important to continue to regularly stash MAW dollars in your INVEST pocket. You can accomplish this by simply redirecting the MAW dollars created by budgeting to the INVEST pocket once you have accumulated sufficient MAW dollars in your SAVE pocket. This way investing becomes a habit, just as saving should be.

Now, we cover the next INVEST pocket decision, "How soon/ How long."

How Soon/How Long?

The INVEST pocket is typically used only for generating money for long-term life goals. These are goals which are more than four years into the future.

The lifelong pursuit of building wealth can often be divided into timetables for particular life goals, such as major purchases, education funding and retirement.

The timetable of an investment is called its holding period—how long you plan to own the investment before hopefully selling it for a profit and converting it to cash. Ideally, the holding period of an investment will suit the timetable of a particular goal. This timing will rarely be perfect, but it is still sound planning to match the holding period in your investment choices with your goal timetables.

Once you have invested the MAW dollars that will eventually fund a goal, you must monitor the investment's performance regularly—monthly, quarterly, annually—to keep the timetable of the investment and the goal in step.

Now that you are aware of the influence of timing on your INVEST pocket decisions, you're ready to deal with the final IN-VEST pocket question—"Where?"

Where?

There are investment opportunities waiting for you at every twist and turn on the Money Ride. The number and variety of choices may seem overwhelming at times, but all investment opportunities will fall into one of six basic categories: business ownership, stocks, bonds, real estate, commodities and collectibles.

Business Ownership

Business ownership means owning your own business, either by your-self or with one or more partners. Any company which is owned by a limited number of individuals where the ownership opportunity is not available to the general public is a "privately held" company.

The incentive for being a business owner is the opportunity to create wealth by growing the value of your business. The value of your business will be based upon its capacity to generate a profit by having more cash flow coming in as income than you have cash flow going out as expenses. The higher your profits, the higher the value of your business.

On the Money Ride, profitable businesses are called "right side up" businesses and unprofitable businesses are called "upside down" businesses.

In an ideal world, your business would be "right side up" all the time, but this is tough to accomplish. In fact, most businesses experience times when they are not generating profits, especially when they are first getting started.

In order to survive and prosper, the unprofitable times must be seldom and brief—on the Money Ride you don't want to get stuck "upside down." As long as your business is operating "right side up," you're earning an income and building wealth.

Passenger Tips & Tools #22

Want to Be an Entrepreneur?

Entrepreneurs play an important role in our society and economy. They are the people who are willing to risk everything they own to create a business, and if they are successful they reap the rewards they deserve.

So, if you want to be one, first go work for one and learn by first being a productive employee. Show initiative, ask questions, watch and learn...it's how many successful business owners start—as a hard-working, productive employee.

In addition to earning an income and building wealth, there are other benefits to owning your own business. As the owner of a company you get to work for yourself. You are your own boss.

As your own boss you have more freedom to do the work you want to do and work the way you want. But with the freedom also comes responsibility and risk—the responsibility of making all the key decisions and the risk of possibly losing everything you have invested in the business.

If you want to be a business owner on the Money Ride, prepare yourself for a special adventure. All the freedom, creativity, uncertainty, excitement and challenge of being a business owner make for a ride that can get wild and crazy at times!

Regardless of whether it offers a product or service, every business operates in its customers' SPEND pocket. As your customers buy your products or services, their SPEND dollars represent revenue to your business. Every revenue dollar you don't spend on the expenses of running your company is a dollar of profit.

As the owner, you can either take profit dollars as personal income or reinvest profit dollars to grow your business. As your business grows, if you manage it well its profits will continue to increase. As profits increase, the value of your business increases—this is how a business owner creates wealth.

Stocks

Stocks and bonds are the most comon investments for employing the accumulation approach to building wealth. However, stocks and bonds are different in what they do and how they do it.

A stock represents a proportional share of ownership in a company organized as a corporation. Corporations can be private or public companies.

Private companies are corporations which usually have a small number of shareholders; the shares are bought and sold privately among individuals. Private corporations are also called "privately-held companies."

Public companies are corporations which usually have large numbers of shares owned by the investing public called "outstanding shares." Their shares are typically bought and sold on public markets called "securities exchanges." Buy-and-sell stock trades are transacted through financial companies known as "securities dealers." Investment firms, banks, insurance companies and financial planning firms typically have a relationship with a securities dealer so that their representatives can sell stocks and other investments to the public.

When you own a company's stock, you own a proportional share of the company's outstanding shares, defined by the market price of a share. As a shareholder, you often have the right to vote on decisions about how the company is run. You also share in the profits and losses of the company. When the share price goes up the value of your investment goes up, and when the share price drops your investment loses value.

The degree of change in a stock's price is called "volatility." A stock whose price change is greater in degree than the change in the overall market is said to be volatile. Regardless of the degree of volatility, these increases and decreases in price and value present opportunity and challenges for investing your MAW dollars in stocks.

In addition to increasing share price, stocks can contribute to wealth-building a second way. Some companies distribute a portion of profits to the shareholders in cash payments called "dividends." Dividends are typically paid annually or quarterly. As a shareholder you have the option to either take the dividend as cash or use it to buy more shares in the company for future growth.

Regardless of whether you invest in stocks for growth or income, you need to have an organized approach to selecting stocks. A selection of stocks is called a stock portfolio and should contain a variety of different types of companies with different growth and risk potential. Having a variety of stocks in a portfolio is called "diversification." Diversification helps to vary the opportunity for growth and spreads the exposure to risk.

Stocks can be grouped into three basic classes, based on company size: large capital, medium capital and small capital. The "capital" stands for the amount of money a company has. Size is important because it is related to the growth and risk potential of a company.

Small companies typically offer the greatest growth upside and risk downside. Small companies have a lot of potential to grow, but they also represent significant risk because they have less capital to weather hard times and stay competitive. This means that you can expect the share price of your small company stocks to experience greater price volatility than the shares of larger companies. Your small company stocks will definitely add some excitement to your Money Ride adventure.

Medium-size companies offer a more moderate degree of growth and risk potential than smaller companies. They may also offer the potential for dividend income. The shares you own in medium-size companies are the middle ground of your diversified portfolio. They offer less risk potential than small company stocks, along with greater growth potential than large company stocks.

Large companies offer less growth potential, less risk and greater long-term stability than small- and medium-size companies. They also offer more potential for dividend income. Your large company stocks will serve as the stable, long-term foundation of your portfolio.

Bonds

Bonds are different from stocks, both in how they work and in the role they play in your INVEST pocket. Bonds are generally considered to have less risk than stocks and are used primarily for safety and income.

 Passenger Tips & Tools #23

Loaner vs. Owner

Remember that you do not invest in bonds for growth. With bonds you are a "loaner" not an "owner." When a bond matures, your original principal is returned to you...before the maturity date you only receive simple interest on your principal, no real growth.

Bonds have an important role in an investment portfolio, but safety and income is what they are used for, not growth.

Like stocks, bonds are bought and sold in the financial markets through securities firms. When corporations and government entities need additional capital for general use or specific projects, they raise the money by issuing bonds which they sell to the public. Owning a bond is like owning an IOU for the money you lend to the issuing entity.

A bond is a promise by the issuing entity to repay the amount borrowed and to pay the bond holder interest for the use of the money. The interest payments are typically paid to the bond holder every six months.

The promise to repay is backed either by the financial strength of the issuing entity or by the income generated by the specific use of the bond proceeds, such as building toll roads and bridges. This financial backing is the bondholder's assurance that the interest will be paid and the debt repaid. If the issuing entity is unable to pay interest or repay the debt, the bondholder has a right to receive repayment from the financial assets of the entity. This financial backing is what gives a bond an added degree of safety over other investments.

A bond works much like a CD except that the term of a bond is longer and the interest paid is usually higher. The term of a bond typically ranges from ten to thirty years, depending upon whether the bond issuer is a company or government entity.

The beginning of the bond term is called the "issue date" and the end of the bond term is called the "maturity date." The bond-holder receives interest payments during the bond term based on the bond's fixed interest rate, called the "coupon rate." For bonds with a term longer than one year, the interest payments are typically made every six months. A bond must be repaid no later than its maturity date. However, a bond may be repaid sooner by the issuing entity if the bond agreement allows.

The interest paid on bonds issued by corporations and the federal government is taxed just like your paycheck, as ordinary income. However, interest paid on bonds issued by city, county and state governments is federal tax-free and state tax-free if you live in the state in which the bond is issued.

A bond's price moves up and down with the prevailing market interest rates. When the prevailing market interest rate rises above a bond's coupon rate, the bond's price drops. When the prevailing market interest drops below the coupon rate, the bond's price rises. You can sell a bond at any time prior to the maturity date to either raise cash or earn a profit by selling at a higher price.

If you hold a bond until its maturity date, the loan is repaid and you get your original investment back. This means that you received interest income during the bond term, but you do not realize any growth on your original investment.

So, if you purchase a stock you are an "owner" and if you purchase a bond you are a "loaner." Owners take more risks and are ultimately concerned with a "return *on* their principal." Loaners, on the other hand, take little or no risk in return for a stable income flow and are ultimately more concerned with the "return *of* their principal."

Now that you know the basics of investing in individual stocks and bonds, it's a good time to learn about an alternative way to build a stock and bond portfolio—mutual funds.

Mutual Funds

Mutual funds are the most popular way to invest in stocks and bonds. You will find that over half of the passengers you meet on the Money Ride invest in mutual funds.

It is important to understand that mutual funds are not a separate type of investment like stocks, bonds and real estate, they are instead what is called an "investment structure." They are a method of packaging an investment product for sale to the public. The package is the mutual fund, and the contents are usually portfolios of stocks and/or bonds.

There are two basic advantages to using mutual funds in your INVEST pocket—diversification and professional management.

Mutual funds operate on the basic principle of diversification. A mutual fund is an investment company which collects MAW dollars from the public and invests the pool of money in stocks and/or bonds. The large pool of money enables the investment company to purchase thousands of shares of hundreds of companies, creating a much larger portfolio than you can as an individual. This allows you to participate in a well-diversified portfolio which spreads risk and expands the opportunity for growth.

Mutual funds employ investment experts who create and manage a large portfolio of individual stocks and bonds on your behalf. The investment management team makes buy-and-sell decisions for you, taking the guesswork out of your stock and bond investment choices.

The mutual fund charges a fee for managing the fund's portfolio. The fee is based on a percentage of the fund's total value and is deducted periodically from the fund's earnings or assets.

When you invest in a mutual fund, you purchase shares in the fund rather than shares of individual stocks or bonds. Mutual fund shares are either purchased and redeemed directly with the mutual fund company or through a stock exchange using a brokerage account.

Every mutual fund has a particular investment objective, which can be defined by the kind of stocks and bonds it owns or by its investment style. The terms "large cap," "international" and "S&P 500 index" are examples of mutual funds defined by what they own. The terms "growth," "value" and "aggressive growth" are examples of mutual funds defined by their management style.

Mutual funds take the guesswork out of picking individual stocks and bonds, but you will still have some homework to do in choosing a mutual fund. You will have thousands of mutual funds to choose from on the Money Ride, and you must base your choices on the funds' objectives, investment styles, management fees and long-term performance record.

 Passenger Tips & Tools #24

Picking a Mutual Fund

Don't chase short-term performance records...look for a fund with a leading long-term performance history.

Look for fund managers who have been with a fund for a long time.

Compare fund expenses and fees...both decrease a fund's gains.

Match the fund's investment objective and risk/reward potential with your investment objectives and risk tolerance.

Real Estate

Real estate is usually a long-term investment, which offers the potential for income and growth. Real estate generates income by charging people rent to use the property. The growth comes from the increase in the market price of a property.

The income and growth potential of real estate is primarily determined by its location. Depending upon its intended use, you want to invest in a property that is located where people want to live, work or play. The current and future economic prospects for the area are also an important consideration.

There are three basic types of real estate. The first type is land, which is property that does not have any buildings on it. The second type is residential real estate, which is property with buildings where people live. The third type is commercial real estate, which is land with buildings where people work.

When investing in land, the goal is either to hold the land for resale or to build something on it. Holding it for resale usually means owning a property for a longer period of time. The hope is that eventually the property's location will attract a buyer who is willing to pay a higher price than you paid for it.

Land can also be purchased with the plan to build a residential or commercial building on the property. The process of buying land and then constructing a building on it is called "developing" and people who do it are called "developers."

As a developer, your goal is to ultimately sell a property for a profit or keep it for its rental income and growth potential.

The more common INVEST pocket opportunity in real estate is to buy an existing residential or commercial property. With an existing property, the initial goal is to generate enough rental income to pay expenses and generate a profit.

Regardless of the type of property you decide to buy on the Money Ride, real estate has an advantage over other investments in how it can be purchased.

OPM

When you buy real estate, the money you pay for it does not all have to be yours. You actually get to use "other peoples' money"— OPM—to pay part of the purchase price of a property. The other great thing about it is that your part of the total price can be a lot smaller than the OPM part. So, where does the OPM come from?

OPM (Other Peoples' Money) is a general term for a loan or debt. OPM can come from individuals or financial institutions. The type of debt used to purchase real estate called a "mortgage loan." You can use a mortgage to buy your personal residence or to buy a residential or commercial rental property which generates income.

You can pay 80% of the purchase price of real estate using a mortgage, and the rest you pay in cash as a "down payment." So, on a $100,000 real property you can "own" it for $20,000 out of your pocket combined with an $80,000 mortgage loan. You start out as a 20% owner with a bank as your partner who owns 80%. All you have to do is make all the payments and you will be a 100% owner.

The bank will loan you as much as 80% or more of the purchase price of the property you want to buy. This purchase loan arrangement with a bank is called "financing."

This means you pay 20% of the purchase price as a down payment and the bank loans you the money to pay the other 80%. You then use the rent income you collect from the property to make loan payments to the bank. The loan payments include repaying the loan, plus an interest charge for the use of the OPM.

Over time, your loan payments will pay off the loan and you will own 100% of the property.

When it comes to reinvesting, real estate has a unique advantage over the other types of investments. With most investments, in order to reinvest cash from profits, you must first pay tax on the profits when you sell the investment to raise cash.

With real estate you can actually take cash profits out of a property without having to sell the property. You also don't have to pay tax on the profit until you ultimately sell the property. This is accomplished by using a strategy called refinancing.

Refinancing is a method of replacing the loan (mortgage) originally used to purchase the property a new loan. The strategy allows you to convert the difference between the original and current value of a property to new MAW cash for reinvesting without paying tax at the time of the transaction. The cash can then be used to purchase a new property to expand a real estate portfolio.

The opportunity to use refinancing, take profits without paying current taxes, gives real estate a special advantage when it comes to reinvesting.

🏍 Passenger Tips & Tools #25

The Real Estate Advantage

Franklin Frugal and Freddy Flash together purchased a rental house in 1997 for $100,000 using a cash down payment of $20,000 and a mortgage loan from a bank of $80,000.

In 2007 the market value of the property had grown to $200,000 and the principal owed on the mortgage was $40,000. Franklin and Freddy decided they wanted to use some of the increased value of the property to buy another house for $200,000 to expand their real estate empire...refinancing was the answer and here is how it worked.

They they needed $40,000 for a down payment and a mortgage loan of $160,000 to buy the new property. So, the refinance of the original property would consist of a new mortgage of $80,000 to pay off the existing mortgage of $40,000 and take $40,000 in cash (new MAW dollars) for the cash down payment to purchase the new property.

Franklin and Freddy now own two houses worth a total of $400,000 with total mortgage debt of $240,000 for a net equity value of $160,000...all created by an initial cash investment of $20,000 on the first house.

Keep in mind that the values, prices, interest rates and percentage of OPM will change, depending on the economy. However, the basic approach to building wealth in real estate is real and always available in your INVEST pocket when the right opportunity presents itself.

Commodities

A commodity is nature's contribution to the world of investments. Commodities are products and raw materials that people buy to satisfy a need or want. A commodity can be an agricultural product like corn, pigs and orange juice or a raw material like coal, gold and oil. Regardless of the type, the prices of all commodities fluctuate based on supply and demand...how many people need or want it (demand) and how much of it is available to buy (supply).

Commodities are growth investments, not income investments. People invest in commodities based on the belief that their price will increase because of a change in supply and demand. This is obviously the same basic reason that people invest in stocks, real estate and businesses. However, since nature has a more direct influence on a commodity's supply and demand than it has on other types of investments, investing in commodities has its own unique aspect of risk and reward...mother nature.

Collectibles

Collectibles are collections of things that have financial value because they are rare or unusual. What makes a collectible item rare or unusual may be a matter of history, art or special interest. Some common examples are art, rare coins, antiques, automobiles, sports memorabilia and books. Collectibles are a growth investment.

Investing in collectibles can be especially risky because the market for buying and selling collectibles is limited to people who have an interest in a particular item. It is also especially risky because people may invest in collectibles for financial reasons, sentimental reasons or both. So, the market for collectibles can be influenced by human nature as well as by supply and demand. Though there are only six basic categories of investments in your INVEST pocket, remember that there are an infinite number of variations within the six categories to choose from.

So, while you're roaring along on your Money Ride adventure keep your eyes and ears open and your imagination alert to the abundant opportunities that await you at every twist, turn, peak and valley.

Read quickly now—two last pockets to learn about before your Money Ride adventure begins.

 **Passenger Watch**

Franklin and Sonya are both feeling pretty good about their recent INVEST pocket decisions. Two of the stocks Sonya has owned for a few years have begun to show promising results. Franklin started a new business with two partners, and they are already profitable thanks to Franklin's frugal grip on the company's cash flow.

Suzie's INVEST pocket is empty, but she has new furniture! Suzie's spending is leading down the path to financial disaster, but she has new furniture!

Freddy is actually doing okay with his INVEST pocket ventures. He does know quality and was smart enough to do his risk/reward homework to make some good stock choices.

8. The Protect Pocket

Expect the Unexpected

There are plenty of potential bumps, bruises and accidents lurking around every corner on the Money Ride—if you're not prepared, they can cost you.

That's why the PROTECT pocket can be the most important pocket on your vest. It's the pocket that "has your back"…that "has you covered." It's the pocket that assures that everything you are trying to achieve financially on the Money Ride won't be derailed by some unexpected loss.

Protection against the risk of unexpected loss is called "insurance," but it really should be called "assurance" because that's what it really provides—the assurance that the wealth-building flow of MAW dollars throughout the pockets on your Opportunity Vest will continue, no matter what unexpected things might happen in your life.

The idea of assurance is important because a loss suffered can generate a negative financial ripple effect throughout the other four vest pockets. Any loss may cause either a direct outflow of SPEND pocket dollars or the ripple effect of having to use SAVE pocket, INVEST pocket—or worse yet—BORROW pocket dollars to cover the loss.

This ripple effect can be as minor as a small additional expense in the SPEND pocket or as serious as entirely stopping the flow of PAW dollars to your vest. Regardless of the degree of loss, an unprotected loss essentially steals MAW dollars from the vest pockets and disrupts the wealth building process.

Health, Income, Property & Life

The four financial domains of potential loss are your health, income, property and life.

Loss of Health

If you have to see a doctor, visit a clinic or go to a hospital because you are sick or injured, you will be charged for any treatment and medicine you receive.

Health insurance is designed to protect you from exposure to medical costs. You will be able to purchase health insurance either under an individual health policy or a group health policy.

You purchase individual coverage personally and pay the entire cost yourself. You can cover yourself as well as your immediate family members under an individual policy.

Group coverage may be available to you if you are a member of a group of people such as employees of a company or a professional association. Group health coverage is purchased through the group, and you typically will only pay a portion of the total coverage cost.

Loss of Income

Except for simply losing your job, income loss is usually caused by an illness or injury. If you are too sick or injured to work, your flow of PAW dollars stops.

Disability income insurance is a form of health insurance that is designed to replace a portion of your income if you are unable to work due to an injury or illness.

This coverage pays a monthly benefit equal to a percentage of your total monthly income, up to a maximum of approximately 66%. The benefit is paid for a stipulated period of time, which varies depending on the type of policy.

Like standard health insurance, you can buy disability insurance using either an individual disability policy or a group disability policy, depending on your situation.

Loss of Property

If any of your personal property, real estate, cars or other assets are damaged or lost, there will be a cost to fix or replace the affected property.

Property and casualty insurance is the type of protection you will need as you accumulate assets on the Money Ride. This type of protection pays the cost to replace or repair property such as cars, homes, furnishings and other valuable assets.

This type of insurance may also offer a special type of protection called "personal liability insurance." It is usually offered as part of the coverage on auto and real property insurance policies. Personal liability coverage protects you in the event you accidentally cause a loss or damage to someone's property. It is especially important protection to have as part of your auto insurance—there are some crazy drivers on the Money Ride.

Loss of Life

When you die, anyone who relies on you financially will lose the income you shared with them or used to support them.

This generally includes family members, but can also include business partners who rely on your contributions to the profitability of the company. It's also advisable to have sufficient life insurance protection to pay off any debts you owe.

Regardless of what type of insurance is involved, in the PROTECT pocket, your decisions will be guided by three basic principles: risk transfer, cost sharing and full replacement value.

Risk Transfer

It is a good idea to transfer risk away from yourself whenever possible. This is what insurance does—you pay the insurance company to assume risk.

Insurance protects your PAW and MAW dollars from the cost of a loss as you rumble along on your Money Ride adventure. For the protection, you will pay the insurance company a fee called a "premium."

Insurance premiums are a fixed expense in your SPEND pocket budget. You can pay insurance premiums annually, semi-annually, quarterly or monthly.

Even if you decide not to buy insurance to transfer a risk, you are still insured, but now you are the insurance company and assume all the risk of loss yourself. It's called being "self-insured." When you are self-insured, you are essentially betting that a certain event is not going to happen.

If you want to be self-insured for any potential loss, you better have a lot of PAW and MAW dollars stashed in your Opportunity Vest. However, if the potential financial loss tied to the event is too great, you may want to reconsider self-insurance and transfer the risk away from yourself…using an insurance company.

Cost Sharing

It is important to know that even if you purchase protection against a potential loss, you won't always be able to transfer 100% of the risk. Depending on the type of coverage you buy, you may have to pay some portion of the cost to repair or replace the affected asset. On the Money Ride, this is called "cost sharing."

The cost sharing portion you pay under the terms of an insurance policy are typically referred to as the "deductible" and may also include "co-pay" or "out-of-pocket" expenses. If a loss occurs, you pay your portion of the cost and the insurance company pays the rest. So, the portion you pay is essentially self-insurance.

Passenger Tips & Tools #26

Deductibles & Reserves

Deductibles are an important tool in controlling the cost of insurance. It is, however, important that you always have sufficient MAW dollars in your SAVE pocket to cover your deductible exposure. So, when you figure your fixed MAW contribution expense in your monthly budget, be sure to factor in the amount of your deductibles.

Depending upon the type of insurance, you usually have a choice as to the amount of the deductible. The higher the deductible, the more you will pay if a loss occurs. A higher deductible also means that it will cost you less to purchase the insurance because you assume more of the risk.

In the PROTECT pocket, the total potential cost for any insurance is the premiums you pay plus the deductible amount you must pay in the event of a loss. This makes cost sharing an important tool for balancing protection needs with protection costs.

Full Replacement Value

The amount of protection purchased to cover any potential loss should be equal to the cost to entirely restore or replace an affected asset. On the Money Ride, this is called "full replacement value" (FRV).

In some cases, FRV may be the money needed to pay expenses resulting from a loss. In other cases it may be the amount of money needed to replace lost income or repair/replace lost property.

FRV is important because if the amount of protection is not sufficient to cover the cost of the loss, then you may have to use MAW dollars or, worse, borrow money to make up the difference. In this way, FRV protects all of your assets, not just the asset directly affected by a loss.

It is important to use FRV to determine the appropriate amount of protection, because it assures that the wealth-building process throughout your Opportunity Vest can continue if an unexpected loss occurs.

Remember that the risk of unexpected loss is lurking in the shadows at every twist and turn along the Money Ride. But do not fear, because armed with the tools of risk transfer, cost sharing and full replacement value, you'll be able to design your own custom-fitted insurance suit of armor to protect you.

Time is growing short—your ride is about to begin. One last pocket left to explore, but it is just as important as the others, so read carefully.

On to the BORROW pocket!

 Passenger Watch

Freddy had a mishap in his new sports car. The car damage is covered, but Freddy is going to be laid up for a while—no work, no income, no disability insurance. He will have to liquidate some of his investments or borrow money to get by until he recovers.

Franklin's company office was damaged by a recent storm. No problem, Franklin made sure when he took over managing the company finances that they had the right kind and right amount of property coverage.

Suzie is shopping for health coverage which is not the kind of shopping she is good at. She's smart enough to know when she is out of her element and has asked Franklin for suggestions.

Sonya has no insurance issues. She has all of her property covered for FRV and has her income and life insured as well. Because she has plenty of MAW dollars in savings and investments, she is able to take advantage of deductibles to keep her premiums low.

9. The Borrow Pocket

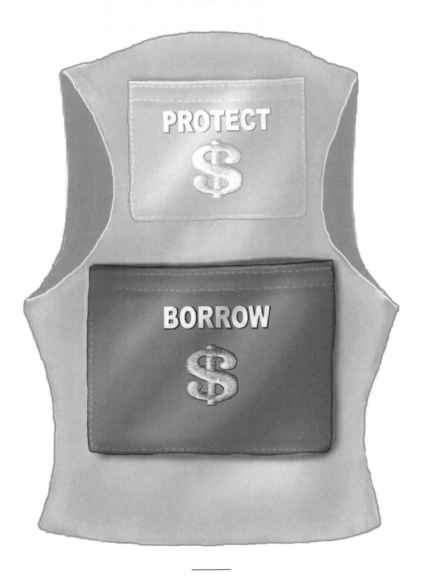

Borrowing: From D^2 to $-S^2$

This is the pocket where you find the money you need to make purchases or investments for which you don't have the cash in your SPEND, SAVE or INVEST pockets. The BORROW pocket on your Opportunity Vest contributes to your efforts to build wealth and enjoy life through smart borrowing decisions.

You probably noticed that the BORROW pocket is so large that it nearly covers the entire back of your Opportunity Vest. It's big because the money decisions you make in this pocket can make a *big* difference in your financial life. This is the pocket where you will have lots of opportunities to succeed and fail, based upon your understanding of what borrowing can do *for* you and what it can do *to* you.

 Passenger Tips & Tools #27

Who Do You Work For?

Having too much debt is like having a second job that doesn't pay you...you pay it.

Some people simultaneously have multiple jobs that cost them instead of paying them. In addition to their regular job, they work for a bank, an auto finance company and one or more credit card companies.

Who do you work for?

In the BORROW pocket, the difference between "for you" and "to you" involves a familiar dynamic you learned about in the SPEND pocket: D^2—discretion and discipline.

Passengers who exercise D^2 are able to make sensible use of their BORROW pocket as a form of $+S^2$ (smart spending) and enjoy an abundant, happy life on the Money Ride.

Passengers who do not exercise D^2 end up using their BORROW pocket as a form of $-S^2$ (stupid spending). As a result, they experience a long, tough, bumpy ride and often find themselves stuck in the Chasm of Financial Despair.

In order to make smart borrowing decisions, you need to remember the three key dynamics of the BORROW pocket:

1. OPM mechanics
2. Your borrowing score
3. Good debt vs. bad debt

OPM Mechanics

You learned a little about OPM (other peoples' money) in the INVEST pocket discussion of real estate. There are many other uses of OPM beyond real estate, which are available in the BORROW pocket. Because of its many potential uses, it's important to understand the mechanics of OPM.

In the BORROW pocket, your sources of OPM may include individuals and financial institutions such as banks, credit unions or credit card companies.

You only get to use OPM dollars temporarily, and then you must pay them back. This temporary use is called a "loan," and all loans are also generally called "debt." A loan is a legal agreement (contract) between two parties to borrow OPM. You are the "borrower" and the source of the OPM dollars is the "lender." The money you borrow is called the "principal" and the fee you pay to borrow the money is called "interest." The unpaid portion of a loan is called the "outstanding balance," and when a loan is entirely repaid it's said to be "paid off." If you are late making a payment you are "delinquent." If you fail to repay a loan you are considered to be in "default" and as far as the lender is concerned, the fault is yours.

There three basic types of debt: revolving credit; installment loans and mortgage loans. Revolving credit is debt that does not have to be repaid each month, but which accumulates interest charges of it is not paid off. Credit cards are an example of revolving credit. Installment loans are debt with a specified dollar amount and repayment period and an agreement to pay back the loan, plus interest, in a series of monthly payments. A car loan is a good example of an installment loan. Mortgage loans, as discussed earlier, are a specific type of installment loan used to purchase real estate.

Every loan agreement has rules governing your use of the money as the borrower. The rules generally cover four main points:

1. How much money you may borrow (loan amount)

The principal amount you are able to borrow will be a function of two factors: your borrowing score and collateral. We will talk about your borrowing score in a minute. First, a brief word about collateral. Collateral can be your income or property you own that the lender has the legal right to take if you don't repay the loan. Most of the time, the property you purchase with the loan is the collateral, such as cars or houses. Other times, you may have to pledge other property as collateral or show proof of sufficient income in order to get a loan.

2. How much you must pay to borrow the money (interest rate and loan fees)

In addition to paying back the principal amount of the loan, you will also have to pay interest. The interest you pay will be based on an annual percentage rate (5%, 6.5% etc.) and each loan payment will include a fraction of the annual interest fee. In addition to the interest charge, there may also be additional fees you have to pay to secure a loan. These are generally referred to as "finance charges" or "loan fees."

3. How much time you have to pay back the loan and the amount of the payments (repayment terms)

Every loan has a repayment schedule which describes the duration of the loan, the frequency of payments and the total number of payments. The payment schedule will tell you exactly the portion of each payment that goes toward repaying the principal and the portion that goes toward paying the interest charge.

4. How you must meet other requirements or conditions of the loan (performance conditions)

Every loan agreement has rules, requirements and conditions which the borrower must satisfy. Penalties for violating the rules can range from paying extra fees and higher interest rates to canceling the loan and requiring early repayment of the outstanding balance.

There are laws governing lending which require certain duties of both the lender and the borrower. Even before the law, common sense suggests that as a borrower you have a special duty to yourself to know exactly what you are in for when you borrow money—know your duties and know your rights.

So, the first rule of smart borrowing is "know the rules" of borrowing before you borrow.

Good Debt & Bad Debt

There are many types of loans available for you to choose from on the Money Ride as you race along. This means your BORROW pocket choices can be tempting, confusing and fast-paced. To keep it simple, remember that all loans represent one of two basic forms of debt—good debt and bad debt.

Good Debt

All good debt has three fundamental characteristics: economic advantage, affordable payments and capacity to repay debt. Debt must have all three of these characteristics in order to qualify as good debt.

In order for debt to have an economic advantage, it must enable you to either save money in your SPEND pocket or make money in your INVEST pocket. This means that good debt either helps you affordably meet important needs and goals or helps you build wealth by acquiring assets.

There may be times when financial emergencies require more money than your PAW income or MAW dollars in reserve can cover. Your ability to borrow the necessary funds to keep your financial stability intact can be considered good debt. An education loan used to earn a degree or learn a new skill in order to earn more income can also be considered good debt. A car loan could likewise be considered good debt if the car is required for earning a living. A home mortgage can also be considered good debt because owning a home builds equity and gives you more control over your lifetime housing expenses by eliminating rent.

Good debt can enable you to make money in your SAVE pocket by funding various opportunities to build wealth by acquiring assets. It could be for real estate or for a business. Whether it is real estate, a business or some other type of investment, good debt is an excellent way to use OPM to create additional income and growth.

The second characteristic of good debt is affordable payments. Affordable payments are payments that fit easily within your monthly budget. This means that the payments do not force you to make drastic changes in your SPEND, SAVE and INVEST pockets, which could compromise your basic lifestyle or cause you to sacrifice important financial goals and opportunities. A good target for keeping debt payments affordable is to try to limit your total monthly debt payments to 25% of your gross income You may not always be able to maintain this limit, but you'll know that if you are over this target, you'll need to adjust your borrowing behavior.

Because your money supply is finite, good debt decisions will require discretion and discipline, D^2. Securing affordable payments should be a top priority with every borrowing decision. This practice will help keep your borrowing score high by keeping debt low and making it easier to make payments on time.

The third characteristic of good debt is the capacity to repay the debt. This means having an adequate supply of PAW and/or MAW dollars to eventually repay the principal amount owed. The capacity to repay is determined by time and money. The longer the term of the debt, the longer you need to continue grabbing PAW dollars and growing MAW dollars until the debt is repaid.

There will be many opportunities for using good debt on the Money Ride; just be sure to use discretion, discipline and the good debt criteria to avoid bad debt.

Bad Debt

No fun—that's what bad debt is on the Money Ride. So, where does it come from and how can you avoid it?

Bad debt is simply debt that does not have all three of the characteristics of good debt. If debt doesn't have an economic advantage, affordable payments and the capacity to be repaid, it is bad debt.

Bad debt comes from a lack of discretion and discipline, D^2 in borrowing decisions, which most often involve the SPEND pocket. This SPEND pocket bad debt is created by simply spending money you don't have. This is accomplished by using OPM to buy things that you don't have the cash to purchase. It may be the payments you can't afford or the total repayment or both—either way you lose because you simply have too much debt.

Credit cards are what most Money Ride passengers use to get themselves in a jam with bad debt. It usually happens with two critical missteps. First, they use credit card OPM to spend cash they don't have.

Second, they fail to pay off the outstanding balance each month.

 Passenger Tips & Tools #28

Hello...Anyone Home?

Having to pay credit card interest on something you want but don't need means paying more for the item than if you simply used cash. This is a really good example of bad debt and $-S^2$, stupid spending. It is also a good example of what is known on the Money Ride as "self-inflicted inflation."

This means that they then have to pay monthly interest on the amount owed until it is paid off. This can in turn lead to the worst situation where the borrower cannot make the required payments and defaults on the loan.

Credit cards are not the only way to get yourself into trouble with bad debt. Any source of OPM which you use to buy stuff you can't afford will have the same *no fun* impact on your Money Ride adventure. It doesn't matter where the OPM comes from or how necessary the item is, any debt you can't afford is bad debt.

On the Money Ride, bad debt is no fun because it takes too many dollars away from opportunities to enjoy life today and to-morrow.

Every dollar of bad debt in your BORROW pocket is wrapped around a heavy brick. The more bad debt you have, the heavier the weight you have to carry on your back. Some passengers become so weighed down with bad debt that they can hardly move. They lose the flexibility needed to keep reaching for PAW dollars. This means that there will be fewer MAW dollars available to take advantage of wealth-building opportunities throughout the pockets on your Opportunity Vest.

Remember that bad debt is like stealing money from yourself, because it eliminates opportunity. The more bad debt you accumulate, the less wealth you'll end up with.

Your ability to make sensible use of debt will enable you to take advantage of good debt opportunities to affordably acquire assets and grow wealth. It will also help you avoid bad debt and all of its limiting and decaying effects on your cash flow and wealth.

Your Borrowing Score

The amount of OPM dollars you will have available to you will depend upon your "credit."

Your credit is your ability to access OPM to buy stuff now and pay for it later. Your credit worthiness reflects your ability to repay debt, which tells a lender how good a risk you are. An important factor in qualifying is your "credit score," which is based on your "credit report."

Your credit report reflects your borrowing history and other details about your borrowing behavior. Credit reports are compiled by firms called credit bureaus, which collect borrower data from financial institutions that issue loans. There are three credit bureaus that compile credit reports: Experion, Equifax and TransUnion.

The FICO score is used most often by lenders. FICO scores are calculated by the Fair Isaac Corporation, FICO. FICO takes borrower data about borrowers collected by credit bureaus and calculates scores based on five factors: payment history; amounts owed; length of credit, new credit and type of credit. Credit scores range from 300 to 850, with a core of 620 considered "good credit" and any score over 720 to be in the "top tier."

You should check your credit report and credit score at least once a year. You are entitled to a free credit report from each of the three credit reporting agencies (Equifax, Experian, and TransUnion) once every 12 months. You can request all three reports at once, or space them out throughout the year.

Your FICO score is like your OPM qualifying exam, and your performance on the exam shows how good of a repayment risk you are. Unlike the exams you take in school, your FICO exam goes on forever. Every time you borrow money for anything, the borrowing event can have an impact on your FICO score.

If your FICO score is high, you are considered a good risk to a lender. If it is low, you're a bad risk. If you want to score high on your FICO exam, keep your debt low in relation to your income, always make payments on time and limit the number of credit accounts in your name.

Money Ride passengers with high FICO scores always have more OPM dollars available than those with low scores. Those with low FICO scores typically are allowed to borrow less OPM and have to pay higher interest rates to borrow it. Some passengers have a FICO score so low that they cannot borrow any OPM.

So, to make the most of OPM opportunities in your BORROW pocket, pay attention to your borrowing habits and keep your FICO score high.

 Passenger Watch

Poor Suzie has so many bricks in her BORROW pocket that she can barely move. Sadly, she can't possibly fulfill her grabbing potential with all the bad debt holding her down.

Franklin is on schedule to pay off his house and retire by age 50. He has no other debt.

Sonya is in no hurry to pay off her house; she would rather have the money in her investment portfolio where it will grow faster than her home's value.

Freddy has realized that his house payment is just too much; it's taking all his fun money to cover it. He plans on finding a smaller place, but he won't leave his exclusive neighborhood—after all, he does have his image to maintain!

10. Time to Buckle Up!

That's it! You now have all the basic information you'll need to make the most of your Money Ride adventure.

Keep this guide close at hand! It will be your handy reference for making the most of the opportunities and challenges waiting for you on the Money Ride.

The time has come! Hurry inside now. Jump into the first empty car you see and buckle up! Get loose and be ready to start grabbing and vesting your lifetime share of Money Ride dollars.

Work hard, work smart, have fun, stay positive and always be alert for opportunities. Be aware of the Money Person you are, and learn from your own and your fellow passengers' Money Ride experiences.

Welcome to the Money Ride—it's the ride of a lifetime, and we are all on it!

Glossary of Money Ride Terms

Bad Debt Any debt that is unaffordable in terms of the payments and/or the repayment.

Borrowing Score Also known as FICO score. Scoring system used to determine a person's credit worthiness based upon their borrowing activity.

Cash Flow Money flowing into the Opportunity Vest as income and out as expenses.

Chasm of Financial Despair The chasm separating PAW and MAW representing the unhappiness caused by the failure to spend less than one earns.

Compounding The accumulation of money created by the continual crediting of interest on principal and on the interest earned in the prior periods.

Financing Borrowing money either to purchase goods and services or to acquire assets.

Fixed Expenses Expenses which reoccur for the same amount each month.

Good Debt Debt which is affordable and which creates a financial advantage.

MAW Money at Work. Excess earnings invested to generated growth and/or income as part of the wealth-building process.

Money Dynamics The roles and rules of money which govern the efficient use of money.

Money I.Q. Knowledge and understanding of how money works and the ability to successfully apply that knowledge to a lifetime of money choices and decisions.

Money Person Personality type described in terms of behavior regarding money.

Money Supply Amount of spendable cash available in the SPEND and SAVE pockets.

OPM Other Peoples' Money; money borrowed using credit cards or loans.

PAW People at Work, generating income by direct labor, a job, work etc.

Ripple Effect The positive or negative effect of one dollar transaction on the other dollars in the money supply.

Risk Tolerance A person's capacity to emotionally and financially assume the risk of loss.

Staging Coordinating the liquidity timeline of various savings vehicles with the timeline of the proposed uses for the money.

Today Dollars PAW and MAW dollars which are needed for current expenses.

Tomorrow Dollars MAW dollars in the SAVE and INVEST pockets designated for future uses.

Variable Expenses Monthly expenses for needs or wants which vary from month to month based on consumption.

Vest Dynamics The mechanics of money affecting the flow of dollars throughout the pockets on the Opportunity Vest.

Work I.Q. All of the education, job skills and personal skills you acquire that enable you to earn an income.

Money Ride Formulas

These formulas and acronyms were created to serve as reminders to help passengers establish and sustain sound money habits.

WORK I.Q. = INCOME • MONEY I.Q. = WEALTH

PAW & MAW • MONEY = COMMODITY

$SCARCITY$ • BUDGET= D^1 • $-S^2$ • $+S^2$

INFLATION / TAXES / SPENDING / MARKETS

SAVE = SAFE • $FV = P(1+i)^n$

INVEST = RISK/REWARD/GROWTH/INCOME

INVEST/DIVERSIFY/REINVEST

<PROTECT >
HEALTH/INCOME/PROPERTY/LIFE

GOOD DEBT
BAD DEBT
OPM • FICO

About the Author

William K. Busch is a financial advisor, educator and public speaker.

Bill has spent the past 27 years helping clients make smart money decisions to address a variety of financial issues and concerns.

He has utilized the diversity of his professional expertise and his background as a business educator to present workshops on personal finance for community groups, companies and schools.

This book is the culmination of his professional experiences working with clients and his years of developing techniques for teaching the fundamentals of money and wealth.

For more information on *The Money Ride*,
and to order additional copies of this book,
please visit

www.TheMoneyRide.com

NOTES

NOTES

NOTES

NOTES

NOTES

NOTES

NOTES